The Group Member's Handbook

D1270032

Frances M. Walsh Consulting
52 Salisbury Avenue
Toronto ON M4X 1C4
[416] 962-8591

The Group Member's Handbook

Strategies for

✓ Great Groups
✓ Meaningful Meetings
✓ Resounding Results

Marilyn MacKenzie and Gail Moore

Published by
Heritage Arts Publishing
1807 Prairie Avenue
Downers Grove, Illinois, 60515

Design: Andrew Moore
Project Management: Penny Manning

ISBN # 0-911029-42-7 The Group Member's Handbook

Partners Plus

Marilyn MacKenzie and Gail Moore are the founding partners in this management consulting firm specializing in training and consulting services to the voluntary and public sectors. This partnership offers the combined strengths of respected and experienced leaders in the field. Their mission is to act as a catalyst in the growth and enhancement of volunteerism in Canada. The firm works with staff and leadership volunteers in national, provincial and local organizations. Partners Plus is the major distributor of voluntary sector publications in Canada and publishes a newsletter, Partners in Print, with subscribers from coast to coast.

Our Services

- ❖ Consultation & Training
- ❖ Keynote Presentations
- ❖ Program Development
- ❖ Distribution of Leading Publications
- ❖ Development of Manuals and Training Programs

Books by Partners Plus

MacKenzie:
Dealing With Difficult Volunteers (1988)
Curing Terminal Niceness (1990)

MacKenzie & Moore:
Building Credibility With The Powers That Be (1990)
The Volunteer Development Toolbox (1993)
The Group Member's Handbook (1993)

9030 Leslie Street, Suite 220, Richmond Hill,
Ontario L4B 1G2, Canada
Telephone (905) 886-8585
Fax (905) 886-9151

Table of Contents

Section A - The Role of The Group Member

Chapter		Page

One Getting Started as a Member **5**

The value of a group; What makes a group successful? Gifts members bring; Duties and obligations; Assessing committee health; Orientation of new members; Sage advice.

Two Member's Orientation to Groups **33**

Orientation to how groups work; Functions of group members; Process and content roles.

Three Learning More About Groups **43**

Verbal participation; Power and influence; Decision-making process; Group norms; Listening skills; Questions to facilitate group activity; Guidelines for giving feedback.

Four Decision-Making in Groups **71**

Types of decisions; Gaining consensus for decisions; Phases of decision-making; Techniques to enhance decision-making; People patterns; Reports and presentations; Dealing with feelings.

Five Resolving Conflict in Groups **89**

Where to start; Principles to resolve conflict.

SECTION B - THE ROLE OF THE LEADER

CHAPTER   PAGE

Six   Leadership   **97**

Practices of exceptional leaders; Parables of leadership; Creative followership.

Seven   Group Leader Task Responsibilities **105**

Task responsibilities; Delegation; Limits of action; Planning for successful meetings; Forms for
effective meeting management; Checklist of meeting leader tasks; Planning the meeting structure;
Building the agenda.

Eight   Group Development   **135**

Stages of group development; Motivating members and creating a team; Recruitment grid; Window of Work.

Nine   Nurturing Individual Members   **153**

Welcoming function; Warm-up activities; Understanding motivation; Coaching; Recognition;
The facilitator's art; Monitoring disruptive behaviours; Tips for improving your chairing skills.

DEDICATED TO OUR SPECIAL MENTORS AND FRIENDS,
SUZANNE LAWSON AND DIANE ABBEY-LIVINGSTON,
WHO TAUGHT US HOW TO LEAD OTHERS WITH COURAGE
AND CARING.

Introduction

Perhaps you're asking yourself, does the world need another book about groups? We think the answer is a resounding YES! As we scan our daily calendars, we are struck by the hours spent in meetings - not just at work but in our busy volunteer lives and even at home. Truth be told, much of this time is wasted time - meetings that lack focus, people who come unprepared, meetings that aren't really necessary but no one has the courage to say ENOUGH!

Make no mistake. We fervently believe in the value of collective wisdom - that people gathered together for a common cause, can make miracles. But miracles don't just happen - they take planning, skill and commitment.

This book is an invitation to great meetings, whether you are a brand new committee member, a new chairperson or a seasoned veteran. As well as the theory behind making meetings successful, we've crammed the book full of practical pointers, observations, worksheets, forms and lots of lively examples. A word of warning. This book is not meant to be devoured whole. Rather like cheesecake, it is best swallowed in small, delicious pieces. We hope you'll return again and again to this book when you're faced with a new group meeting challenge.

Gail Moore & Marilyn MacKenzie
Partners Plus, 1993

SECTION A

THE ROLE OF THE GROUP MEMBER

CHAPTER 1
GETTING STARTED AS A MEMBER

THE VALUE OF THE GROUP

There's a lot of talk about the ineffectiveness and inefficiency of groups. Groups are the constant target of lots of humour:

> A camel is a horse designed by a committee.

> A meeting is a gathering where people speak up, say nothing, then all disagree.

That said, there is still enormous potential in the work of a group, for at the heart of all group effort is the belief that a collection of people can develop better solutions to life's problems than a single soul working alone. Why is this so?

❖ Groups bring together people with different sets of skills, interests and perspectives to work on problems of joint concern.

❖ Groups, when they work well, experience a release of energy and creativity that builds unique solutions. The result is truly greater than the sum of the parts.

❖ Involvement in the development of plans and solutions builds commitment to the results. When people have built a solution, they are more likely to support it and to work for its implementation.

❖ When groups include representatives of those affected by the issue, they are often able to consider a broader range of important aspects of the problem under discussion.

❖ Relationships developed at the committee table can enrich our own lives both personally and professionally.

WHAT MAKES A SUCCESSFUL GROUP?

If your own experience suggests that many groups waste time and achieve little, what's different about a successful group?

A successful group has the following characteristics:

- ❖ clearly defined, mutually agreed-upon goals and objectives

- ❖ a positive, supportive climate that encourages everyone to participate

- ❖ members who listen attentively to one another

- ❖ ideas that are fully and candidly expressed

- ❖ flexibility in approaching problems

- ❖ responsiveness to all group members

- ❖ high standards of performance for the group and each of its members

- ❖ a sense of community that produces synergy in its work

- ❖ the welcomed expression of diverse points of view, acknowledging that conflict can provide an opportunity for new insights to be developed

- ❖ evaluation of both the product and process of its effort, to improve future performance

- ❖ recognition of the unique worth of each member of the team, valuing the contribution of all.[1]

THE GIFTS GROUP MEMBERS BRING

To contribute fully, the greatest gifts a member can bring to a committee or group are:

❖ A sincere commitment to work on behalf of the issue under discussion.

❖ The time available to serve, not only at the meetings, but in between to read and think about the issues raised.

❖ An appreciation of the possibilities. Groups have at their disposal a rich mix of resources that individuals bring with them when they join, if the group will permit those potential resources to be tapped.

❖ The basic skills of membership - listening, feedback, questioning and participation.

❖ An understanding of how groups work and what behaviours will enhance the ability of the group to work effectively together.

These skills and attitudes are not magical, complex or unattainable. On the contrary, major improvements in group satisfaction and group performance can be achieved by the application of a few simple tools and techniques. Any member can make a difference in the success of the group.

DUTIES AND OBLIGATIONS OF MEMBERS

If the gifts the member brings include enthusiasm, commitment and some basic skills, what are the duties or obligations inherent in group membership?

1. At the very least, it is to attend the meetings.

One technique that can greatly increase the likelihood of full attendance, is to prepare, in concert with the group, a year long schedule of dates and times of meetings. Consider the preferences of group members for dates, times and perhaps, location. Setting a date that is unsuitable for any participant suggests that the person's involvement is unnecessary or unimportant. Everyone must be accommodated. The complete list of meetings might be reproduced on a heavy stock paper, suitable for keeping in a date book, on a fridge door or mounted on a bulletin board.

A second practice that will reduce absenteeism is to send a reminder notice of the meeting at least ten days before the scheduled date. This is an opportunity to pre-circulate the agenda, pre-discussion background papers and instructions for items to be considered.

Participation means a lot more than being physically present. It is an active involvement in every aspect of the work of the committee. It includes planning, discussion, development of alternatives, coming to conclusions, supporting those conclusions with the local constituency and working to implement decisions taken.

Traditionally, it has been the leader who bears responsibility for creating the conditions and employing the processes that would encourage others to participate. Today we recognize that this responsibility is best shared so that all group members have a part in shaping the results of group effort. Good committees welcome shared leadership.

What does this say for the "quiet member", the one who prefers to listen rather than talk? The question is not one of quantity (everyone must speak three times on every agenda item), but of quality. Is the member contributing to the work of the group? Different styles of participation are valid, as long as the opinions of all members are actively sought and factored into group decision-making. This may require that a quiet participant take an unaccustomed assertive stance to voice concerns or suggest a new approach.

2. Meetings are forums for strong feelings, vigorous debate and lively interchange, not a platform for endless reporting back on events of the past or declarations of how things will be done. Unfortunately, some meetings lose sight of the opportunity presented when people gather. Expect sparks, differences and passion. It is the very essence of a good meeting. But time must be allotted and the groupings of people must permit frank talk. Large meetings can be regularly broken down into small discussion groups, to consider proposals, to evaluate suggestions. In this way, everyone is obliged to keep alert and think through implications. The large group is then reconvened, with an opportunity for feedback, further reflection and final decision-making.

3. Keep an open mind. If you are unable to respond to a persuasive argument or to change your opinion as a result of new information, your participation on the committee is of diminished value. You might as well have sent an envelope with your vote. Today we see a proliferation of single issue people who demand representation on boards and committees. They come, not to participate as full committee members, but rather to use the resources, connections and credibility of the committee as a platform for their own point of view. Their genuine interest is not to the work or health of the committee, but rather the spreading of their own issue's propaganda. Their involvement is beneficial only when their ends are congruent with the achievement of wider goals.

A classic example is the demand of right-to-life groups to be seated on hospital boards. They present themselves at Annual

Meetings with a single concern, to prevent abortions from being performed at a hospital. If they are elected, during their term they pursue only their declared objective. They are uninterested in the other business of the hospital and may fail to attend meetings when abortion is not on the agenda.

4. Acting on behalf of the whole requires courage and an appreciation of the bigger picture at the expense of local interests. This dilemma plagues representatives who feel compelled to vote as their backhome constituents see fit. We need to release members to vote as they see fit, given firstly their understanding of the backhome situation, but with understanding of the broader issues involved and with access to further information and advice. It is a serious weakening of the group process. The exposure to different points of view should broaden our own perspective and deepen our understanding of others.

This does not preclude, of course, your arguing strongly for your own point of view. You have an opportunity to persuade and influence. But your position must be responsive to what benefits the whole group, not just your special interest. That's the essence of responsible committee membership.

5. Embedded in your role as a group member is an obligation to make the group work, to make it stronger. You, along with your fellow group members, become caretakers of the group as a whole and of each individual within the group. This commitment does much to eliminate those destructive behaviours that get in the way of effective group action - the games of one-upmanship, the power tripping, the withdrawal from important decisions, the belittling of any individual. Energy is best focused on finding out what others need to bring the group to agreement.

6. In a group that works to achieve consensus, decisions made cease to be the work of one individual, but become the property of the full group. There are no winners or losers. Because everyone is involved in its creation, everyone is comfortable with the result. The fierce debate that raged inside the group has been resolved and the group speaks with one voice.

When agendas are packed full or people are impatient to move forward, controversies are not fully explored. Debates are cut short and a premature vote takes place. This creates incredible resistance for the "losing side". These people feel alienated from the other members and the decision. They cannot speak to the result with conviction. The speed gained in a quick resolution is lost in the resentment felt and the trust destroyed. The quick victory is an illusion, for the long-term cost will far outweigh the perceived benefit of time saved.

7. As a committee member you are asked to develop a consuming passion for the issue under discussion. Exhaust your local resources to get information. Seek out alternative sources to see the issue through different eyes. Talk to people, consult experts, scan the papers, invest your time in becoming knowledgeable.

8. Very few issues lie dormant waiting for your intervention. They grow, develop and change while you are considering them. Be sure that your solutions match the changing realities in your community.

9. Getting to know your fellow group members as people, not just as cardboard figures across a table, is a worthwhile endeavour. Insight, respect and understanding come with increased knowledge.

Even experienced group members benefit from training when a new group forms, for each group is a new start, a new set of variables and challenges. Retreats allow you the luxury of reflection, social interaction and guided practice (a chance to test out new ways of behaving under the watchful eye of an experienced facilitator).

10. Even great groups can do better! Evaluation is a time to celebrate:

- accomplishments
- enhanced decision-making
- improved relationships

This is a time to take stock. What might we do better? How can we streamline our efforts? How do we support our new members? Write better background papers? Report our progress?

Evaluation should not be done only once a year, but can be built into every meeting. Kayser [2] speaks of the process check - how are we doing? What needs alteration? How far have we come? (More on this later).

Creating a climate that welcomes regular evaluation as an opportunity for growth is a positive force for effectiveness.

The Duties of a Group Member

1. Attend and participate in all group meetings.

2. Come to meetings prepared to listen, ponder, debate and question.

3. By all means come with a point of view, but be prepared to change it if the evidence suggests change is in order.

4. Always be prepared to act in the best interests of the total organization, not just a single interest or distinct geographical region.

5. Use your role on the group to build group strength, to facilitate decision-making with which everyone can feel comfortable.

6. Once a vote is taken and a decision is reached, act as a spokesperson on behalf of the group as a whole to explain and defend the final position of the group, even if you originally objected.

7. Stay informed about issues related to the work of the group, building your knowledge and understanding of all sides of the issue.

8. Keep abreast of changing needs in your constituency and see that those are reflected within the group.

9. Support efforts to enhance group effectiveness and efficiency by participating in training, social activities and retreats.

10. Welcome evaluation.

An Invitation to Join a Group -
the Questions to Ask

Domenic was surprised when he received an invitation to sit on a community-based environmental group. He had worked successfully on the Parents' Council at his local school and had just finished a productive term as Vice-President of the Minor Hockey League in his home town. But he'd never done anything for the environmental movement. Rumours around town suggested that this group was in trouble. Domenic always looked for a challenge, but frankly, he didn't know how to decide. Should he accept the offer to serve?

Questions To Ask Yourself

Before you agree to sit on a committee, you should consider the following questions:

- Do I have a passionate interest in this issue?

- Am I able to devote the time to participate wholeheartedly:

  - during the meetings?
  - in preparation for meetings?
  - in the work generated by decisions taken?

■■■■■■■■

Questions to Ask the Chairperson of This Committee or Group

When you are approached to serve on a committee, here is a list of questions you might pose to the chairperson or to the recruiter.

- What is the purpose of this group?

- What are the goals and objectives?

- What are the timelines and action plans?

- What are the terms of reference?

- What is the nature of my time commitment to this committee?

  - term of office
  - number of meetings with dates
  - amount of work in preparation as a result

- What other obligations are involved in sitting on this committee?

Considering The Answers

Unless you are passionately committed to the focus of the group's effort, it is unlikely that you will invest the needed energy and enthusiasm to get the job done. You may feel that you are letting down the individual or organization asking you to join. In fact, though, by saying no, you open up the opportunity for someone who may be actively committed to the issue.

The time question is not as simple as it first appears. Often recruiters try to persuade participation by claiming "It's only three meetings a year". This artificially minimizes the work that goes on behind the scenes in preparing to attend the meeting (pre-circulated materials, ad hoc task forces, preparation of reports, background documents) and between meetings (the lobbying of group members, the meeting with constituents, the investigation of other points of view). In most situations, the meetings represent only a small fraction of the real work done by the committee. Try to get a feel for the actual time that will be spent in between meetings.

Often membership on one committee implies participation in other work groups that explore options and then take action to implement the decision. Being clear about the full range of obligations that an agreement to participate brings, allows a member to give fully informed consent.

The answers given by the chairperson are equally as important. Purpose gives the group focus, energy and direction. Successful groups need a clearly defined purpose that has been reviewed and amended by the full group. In the absence of purpose, a group spends much of its time in confusion, uncertain of its direction or destination. Occasionally, the chairperson has a clear sense of where he wants the group to go, but without their explicit approval, they will not meet his expectations.

The second set of questions speaks to the planning process in the group. Does the group have the "right stuff" to move to action? Every group needs to outline who is doing what, when, with what resources. These plans should be written, widely shared and the basis for meeting agendas and activities during the life of the group. Rather than a straitjacket to limit action, the plans offer a road map that permits delightful side trips, if needed. Without direction, there can be no momentum.

The terms of reference referred to in the third question relate to boundaries of action. For good advice on developing terms of reference, you may want to read *Chairing a Committee* by Ginette Johnstone[3]. What is expected of this group? To whom do people report? What are the resources they bring, what is the composition of the group? Whom does it serve? The terms of reference provide a mini-orientation to the prospective member about who we are, where we fit, what we do and with what result.

Committee Terms of Reference

Committee Name:_____

Committee Reports To:_____

Purpose:_____

_____

Timeframe:_____

Duties:

      1._____

      2._____

      3._____

      4._____

      5._____

Chair:_____

Membership:_____

_____

_____

Resources (budget, staff):_____

Notice of Meetings:_____

Quorum:_____

MANDATORY MEMBERSHIP

Occasionally you may be assigned to a committee that is not of interest to you, but is an obligation. This mistake is often made by employers or organizations when they feel the need for a "presence" at the table. If you find yourself in this circumstance, you need to create your own commitment. Identify for yourself:

- ❖ the unique purpose for your presence

- ❖ the clear benefits that this committee might provide you, your community and your special interest group

- ❖ the shared goals that your constituency can achieve by supporting the work of this committee.

Try to create a raison d'être for your involvement that allows you to work on behalf of the committee and meet your own needs and interests at the same time.

These days many prospective committee members now request an opportunity to sit in on a meeting and observe how the group functions before they agree to serve. This is a great idea because it allows the potential member to assess the key factors that determine group health. Consider using the following chart to guide your observation:

A Checklist for Assessing the Committee's Health

1. The Climate
- ☐ Does it feel warm, supportive and friendly?
- ☐ Are some parts of the group hostile or resistant?
- ☐ Is the atmosphere comfortable or tense?
- ☐ Are you introduced to all other committee members and made to feel welcome or are you ignored?

2. Interaction
- ☐ Does the chairperson recognize others or maintain a stony silence?
- ☐ Is the meeting one of sharing or is it a one-way monologue?
- ☐ Is all participation directed at the chairperson or is there lively debate involving everyone?
- ☐ Are there cliques? (small groups who appear to carry on their own meeting)
- ☐ Are there silent members?

3. Conflict
- ☐ Is conflict acknowledged and explored or suppressed and denied?
- ☐ Are different points of view welcomed?
- ☐ Does the committee identify a range of options or adopt the first suggestion?
- ☐ Are there obvious winners and losers in discussions?

4. Decision-Making
- ☐ Are decisions made or is discussion circular, without resolution?

5. Energy
- ☐ Do you sense enthusiasm, excitement, passion - or is the group flat, unresponsive?
- ☐ Are there flashes of humour, intensity?

6. Evaluation
- ☐ Is the process or the product ever evaluated? Does the group spend time looking at its own performance?

Before saying yes to an invitation to participate, a prospective member should consider carefully the results observed in the key six areas. Sometimes, the purpose of the group is so personally compelling (a chance to eliminate hunger, to work of behalf of peace, to improve community health, to appoint a new leader) that you are willing to overlook poor group performance in order to get involved. Do so with the clear understanding that progress will be slow unless the performance issues are resolved.

WHAT'S AN INDIVIDUAL TO DO?

Marion had received an invitation to sit on the Mayor's Task Force on Hunger and she was enormously excited and proud. Of course, Marion had sat on committees before but this was different. This was an issue that really mattered and Marion wanted to do - not just a good job - but a great one! As Marion thought about her role as a committee member, she acknowledged that she knew very little about what makes great groups and so she decided that she really wanted to find out.

Marion has been asked to sit on a committee dealing with an issue she believes in. She is anxious to do well. What must Marion do to move from an enthusiastic newcomer to a well-accepted veteran committee member?

Committee Member's Orientation Checklist

Print Resources

As part of her orientation, Marion needs to become familiar with the following items. Preparing a binder that includes these print resources would be useful

- ☐ The terms of reference.
- ☐ The purpose of the committee.
- ☐ Goals, objectives, action plans to date.
- ☐ Last year's minutes.
- ☐ Reports and products produced by the committee in the last two years (for example a manual or guidebook).
- ☐ Items under study or review.
- ☐ Committee membership list - phone numbers, addresses, short written bios would be ideal.

Human Resources

To complete her orientation, Marion needs to arrange the following one-to-one discussions. Note that the new recruit must take the initiative to orient herself if the chair fails to do it.

- ☐ Meeting with the chairperson.
- ☐ Optional meeting with staff.
- ☐ Introduction to mentor or buddy.
- ☐ Introduction to committee members.

General Orientation

These are sample interest areas for new committee members. There may be others in your agency that need to be included

- ☐ Pertinent polices and practices.
  - How to complete the expense forms for:
    expenses
    meals
    telephone and courier
    parking
- ☐ Tour of building
- ☐ Orientation to organization
- ☐ Confidentiality policies
- ☐ An introduction to group norms.

1. The terms of reference

2. The purpose

3. Goals, objectives and action plans

4. Last year's minutes

This information gives you an in-depth account of the work accomplished by the group, a sense of who is doing that work and the issues under attention. Understanding the history prepares you to contribute to the future of the group.

5. Reports and products produced by the committee.

Reports alert you to the issues and decisions that the committee believes are important. They highlight accomplishments and future plans. Products are the children of committee effort. You can learn much about the unstated beliefs of a committee by reviewing the products they produce. What do manuals, brochures, buttons, tell you about the target market of the committee, the thrust of the message, the solutions they propose, the nature of the help they offer? Do the products correspond to the stated committee goals and objectives? What gaps still exist?

6. Items under study or review.

What documents are the group using to make decisions and to take action? Where are the sources of information? Who are the authorities in the topic under study? How do I prepare a balanced set of recommendations? What is the opposition saying about the topic? There is a great temptation to read only those documents that support one's own belief system. It is important to understand the opposing side's arguments in order to prepare a convincing rebuttal.

7. Committee membership list.

Full participation in the committee is greatly facilitated when members' full names, addresses and phone numbers are made available to each member. Ideally, a short biography with a picture seals the connection for everyone.

8. Meeting with the chairperson.

It is very helpful to schedule an informal get-together with the committee chairperson. It allows the chair to get to know you in order to introduce you and give a bit of background to the group about the reason you were selected for membership. Approval by the chair lends credibility and status to your participation, easing your transition into the group and speeding your acceptance.

Meeting the chairperson allows you to begin the building of your relationship with him. It is an opportunity to identify shared objectives and to observe the chairperson's style. You will be able to determine what the chair values and how he will conduct the meetings.

9. Meeting with staff.

Spending time building a positive relationship with the staff person supporting committee effort is a wise investment. Staff are often gatekeepers of the larger organization's resources and they know how to access needed resources (audiovisual equipment, typing and duplicating, expense forms, mechanisms for gaining approval of recommendations). The staff person is a full partner in the work of the committee and should be accorded the respect and thoughtfulness accorded any other member.

10. Introduction to a mentor or buddy.

One of the most effective resources in an orientation program is a buddy or mentor. The role of the buddy is to act as a liaison, introducing the member to others. She can also explain procedures and current committee practices. There are benefits for the person selected as a mentor. This selection recognizes exemplary effort on the part of the buddy. Because of their fine record and commitment they are asked to be a role model for newer members and to show them the ropes. A mentor can play an important role in validating the experience of the new member for the full committee. It might be appropriate to suggest that the buddy call the member before the meeting, ensuring transportation and answering questions.

11. Introduction to all committee members.

The new member will feel more at ease if she has a chance to talk briefly with every other member of the committee. The buddy can initiate the introductions, offering a tidbit about the new member and about the committee member that will build a relationship. A new member should be encouraged to sit next to different people at meals, during breaks and in discussion to build relationships with all of the group.

12. Pertinent policies and practices.

The new member will need to be informed of those policies and practices that directly affect him. These might include:

❖ Expense Practices: What items will be reimbursed and which forms must be completed?

❖ Meal Allowance: What meals are provided? Costs? Recommended places to eat?

❖ Parking: Where is recommended? How are costs handled?

❖ Telephone and Courier Costs: Is a calling card provided? Is there an 800 number? How are emergencies handled?

❖ Confidentiality: Committees often discuss sensitive material that is not yet ready for public knowledge.

Members need to appreciate the importance of confidentiality during committee deliberations so that discussions can be full and frank. To ensure compliance, many committees encourage members to sign a pledge of confidentiality. A useful addition to this practise is the introduction of role plays that display common situations where confidentiality is breached. An opportunity to talk over these situations with a knowledgeable colleague or small group increases the likelihood that the concept will be honoured.

13. Tour of the facility.

If the member is new to the organization or the physical plant, you may want to include a tour of the building as part of the overall orientation. Knowing where the cloakroom is, how to get a cup of coffee, where office supplies are kept, and who operates the building is an important aspect of personal comfort. One important person who is often neglected on a facility tour is the receptionist. Making sure the member is acknowledged and recognized whenever she enters the facility, goes a long way to extending a warm welcome.

14. Orientation to the organization.

Committee members often serve without prior knowledge of the organization. To enhance performance, they will benefit from a clear notion of:

- purpose of the larger organization
- where they fit in an organizational chart
- who their staff partners are
- the structure of the organization
- a brief history.

The key to success here is to keep it brief and focused on what the individual needs to do his best work on behalf of the agency.

Although an orientation should be a routine part of any new committee member's first encounter with a group, you may discover nothing has been planned. In that case you must set out to secure the necessary information to orient yourself. The support probably exists, but has not been brought together for your ease. The Orientation Checklist will direct you to what you need.

Orientation when everyone is new should involve considerable time spent getting to know one another. When a group is brand new, people feel uncomfortable and uncertain - "Will I fit in?" "Will my opinion matter?" "Am I as knowledgeable or experienced as everyone else?"

During this period, there is very little listening going on because people are focused on their own discomforts. By taking time to help people feel more comfortable with one another and to stress the similarities and strengths each member brings to the table, it is possible to build a team and start the task work of the group.

Often, the relationship building is best begun by allowing people to pair up with others to talk about shared interests.

This exercise is not, as some see it, wasted time, but helps people establish a relationship with at least one other person. It allows people to identify their own competence and commitment and helps them see the potential contribution of others. Anxiety and uncertainty are dimmed and people are able to focus on the task of the group. Taking time at the front end of a committee pays dividends in the long term. When committee members know and value one another as people, conflict is reduced and members commit themselves to working on behalf of the full group, not just themselves.

A Getting to Know You Exercise

Encourage people to pair up with one other person on the committee. Allow 20 minutes for this sharing. You may then want to have each partner introduce the other to a second couple or move to the full group.

Name:_____

Position/Title/Agency: _____

The purpose of this Committee is:_____
_____

The reason I'm interested in the work of this Committee:_____
_____
_____

One thing I'd like to see happen is:_____
_____
_____

One thing I don't want to see happen is:_____
_____
_____

In my spare time, one hobby I especially enjoy is:_____
_____

THE NEW KID ON THE BLOCK

It is usually difficult to join a group already in progress. You are an outsider. If the committee has been underway for some time, you will want to review the essential background material as outlined in the Committee Member's Orientation Checklist. You will find it easy to acquire the needed print resources to "bring you up to speed." Despite your best efforts, however, you may find group members reluctant to grant you full committee membership status. This is evidenced for example, when:

- you are not introduced to the group
- the comments you offer are ignored
- there is loud objection to a suggestion you make
- you find yourself standing alone during refreshments
- your availability to attend the next meeting is not considered when selecting a date.

A colleague offered this sage bit of advice: "When you're new, wear beige and smile a lot."

Trust and inclusion are not automatic with an invitation to join a committee. Use the first three or four meetings to listen intently and to ask clarifying questions about the work previously done. You will not be a very effective change agent during the early stages of your membership, as you lack credibility and history with your peers. If you see areas for improvement, write them down for future implementation but consider the focus of this time to be building your own learning curve.

Sage Advice for the New Member

1. Listen, listen, listen. Find out what people think, where they would like the committee to be, their dreams and demons.

2. Ask clarifying questions:

> What do these initials mean?
> What is the usual practice in receipting donations?
> How did you become interested in this agency?

Notice there is no implied criticism of how things were done a certain way. Consider yourself in the DATA GATHERING phase, with no evaluation or judgment at this time.

3. Demonstrate respect for past efforts and especially the people who have led the organization or your committee in the past.

4. Support suggestions of others when you feel they are sound. Identify one or two things you like about the suggestion, clearly crediting the development of the proposal to the other person.

> "I think Bob has a great idea. I especially like the inclusion of spouses for our appreciation dinner."

> "I'd like to speak in support of Jennifer's motion. We need to be seen at local events more often. The increased community profile makes a lot of sense."

5. When you are evaluating the comments offered by an established committee member, practise the itemized response technique.

Before you level any criticism of another's viewpoint, identify two specific things you like about the proposal. That done, identify one aspect you might change. Be careful how that item is presented - instead of being negative or critical, try to focus on your wish for the outcome.

Not this:

"This idea needs a lot of work. The title is wrong, I've got my doubts about a Saturday/Sunday thing and the mailing list is incomplete."

Examples:

"I'm excited about the location of the Bingo and the partnership with the Lion's Club, but my wish would be for a non-smoking event."

"I love the idea of new uniforms for the Little League teams, especially from this supplier. My hope would be that we can share the costs with the parents through fundraising projects."

"I think the format and design layout for the Amateur Theatre Night brochure is right on. I'd love to see a bright, show-stopping colour added to the text."

Your purpose here is to have your ideas heard. In acknowledging specifically what you like, you build allies who view the world as you do. You clarify your points of agreement and introduce a single point of departure as a wish that the listener may choose to consider. Such a placement and wording invites a positive response.

6. Present ideas as questions or tentative proposals rather than should-do's or must act.

Not this:

"When I was with Girl Guides, we did it this way and it worked very well." (Invites the response "But this isn't Girl Guides ...")

But rather:

"What would happen if we increased the fees to $75.00 per person? What fall-out do you anticipate?"

"How would the public respond if we changed the picnic site to a national park instead of the private site?" (Invites the response "Let us together consider this option")

7. Identify your unique contribution to the proceedings. Be prepared to offer that to the full group.

REFERENCES

1. Adapted from *The Team Building Source Book*, Steven L. Phillips and Robin L. Elledge, University Associates, San Diego, 1989.
2. Kayser, Thomas, *Mining Group Gold,* Pfeiffer and Company, 1990.
3. Johnstone, Ginette, *Chairing a Committee, A Practical Guide*, 1989.

CHAPTER TWO
MEMBER'S ORIENTATION TO GROUPS

To function effectively, a committee member should develop an understanding of how groups work. There are two dimensions to any group meeting - the content and the process. The content includes the task to be done:

- raise $10,000 for a new piece of equipment
- elect a board president
- plan a recognition dinner
- develop a program after school.

Content concerns include all the activities, plans, objectives and proposals that move you toward the resolution of your stated goal.

The process component deals with how people participate in the discussion and the decisions. While the content piece of group functioning is very evident when observing the group, the process component is less obvious. That doesn't mean it isn't just as important.

The process functions relate to:

- how people feel about their role on the committee
- their relationship with others in the group
- relationship between the chairperson and the members
- how conflict is handled
- how decisions are made.

A delicate balance between the achievement of content and process goals must be maintained if a group is to move ahead. A beginning committee member needs information not only about the topic at hand, but also about the group in which he becomes a member.

Sharing the Process and Content Roles

As the group sets about learning to work effectively together and tackles the project for which it was formed, certain roles emerge. Traditionally, the group leader has been in charge of moving the group forward on both the process and content issues. No longer. Now every member is encouraged to know the roles that must be undertaken and to step in when she sees an unmet need. The task or content roles help the group achieve its goals and solve problems. The process roles help the group relate more sensitively to one another, building relationships so they can work together more productively.

Content Roles (Tasks)

1. Defines Problems

A member contributes to the identification, analysis, definition or outline of a group problem:

> Examples:

> "What I see as the main issue here is that we need permanent staff."

> "We have three options to follow:
> we cut back on expenses
> we engage in an aggressive fundraising campaign
> or we do both things at the same time"

2. Seeks Information

A member requests factual information about the group problem, method, procedure or for clarification of a suggestion.

> Examples:

> "Help me understand why you've come to that conclusion?" ·

"If we cut expenses, will we have to give up our new office space?"

3. GIVES INFORMATION

A member offers facts or information about a group problem, methods to be used, clarifies a suggestion.

Examples:

"We know that 15% of the children who call the help line are under age 12."

"We could call for a vote because we have a quorum here today."

4. SEEKS OPINIONS

An individual asks for opinions of others relevant to the discussion.

Examples:

"Bob, what's your advice on the logging issue?"

"Marion, you've spoken strongly on this issue before. What's your read here?"

5. TESTS FEASIBILITY

A member questions reality, checks practicality of suggested solutions.

Examples:

"Is the sense of the meeting that we are ready for a vote?"

"Are you suggesting we end funding to the group, Ted?"

Process Roles (Relationships)

1. Coordinating

The member clarifies a statement and relates it to another statement in such a way to bring them together. Reviews proposed alternatives.

> Examples:
>
> "Building on Bob's statement, I'd like to suggest we can offer free concerts and still provide quality programming."
>
> "I think Mary is right. I'd like to see us plan for additional space for campers next year."

2. Mediating/Harmonizing

A member highlights similar views, interceding in disputes and disagreements, attempting to reconcile them.

> Example:
>
> "Perhaps your views are not so different. Both of you support extensive fundraising efforts. You just have different targets. Could we do both?"

3. Orienting/Facilitating

The member keeps the group on track, points out deviations from agreed upon rules and procedures. Helps group process, proposes group procedure to make the group more effective.

> "That's an interesting comment, Jennifer, but how does it relate to our goal of getting music into the school curriculum?"

"We have about fifteen minutes left before lunch. Perhaps we can use the time to summarize the key concepts we agree upon this morning."

4. SUPPORTING/ENCOURAGING

Expresses approval of other's suggestions; is warm and responsive to other's ideas, verbal and non-verbal.

Examples:

"Please go on. (Nodding of head, leaning forward) That's a great idea. Tell me more about it."

5. FOLLOWS

The member goes along with the movement of the group; accepts ideas of others; expresses agreement, serves as audience during discussion.

Examples:

"Okay, Penny, I think I see what you have in mind."

"Hey, I think we're on the right track here."

All group roles are necessary but different roles are required at different times. You might expect that seeking and giving information might be seen more extensively in the early stages of group work while testing feasibility might be more likely at a later stage of development.

A balance of both task and group maintenance functions is required to get work done. Very often, task issues are dealt with, leaving the group maintenance functions unattended. The group fails to bond as a group and the full participation of members is never achieved.

Unless consciously attempted, group member interventions can be haphazard and self-serving. Hedley Dimock [1], an expert in group dynamics suggests that by observing group interaction, group members can determine:

- which roles are not being addressed
- who fulfils which roles
- who dominates
- who does not participate.

The group can then agree to:

- share the necessary roles
- introduce missing elements into group process
- practice new skills.

In this way, each member can develop a larger repertoire of group roles and can enhance her skill and comfort in using them.

INDIVIDUAL BEHAVIOURS

These behaviours help the individual meet his own needs at the expense of the group. It's helpful to know what individual behaviours are and to recognize them when they occur. Help to lessen their impact is discussed in Chapter Nine.

1. BLOCKING

Interfering with the progress of the group by arguing, resisting and disagreeing beyond reason. Returning to an issue that has already been settled.

Examples:

"I'm still not satisfied with the decision taken at the last meeting. It needs to be back on the agenda" (The rest of the group roll their eyes)

"Because I say so. We've never done it that way and I'm completely in opposition."

2. Digressing

Consistently leads discussion away from issue at hand and into an area of personal interest. Delivers long, unfocused speeches.

Examples:

"Why I remember how it used to be here. We were a family, never a cross word spoken, never a debate! We always resolved our problems peacefully. Why, only last week I was speaking to Joe. He used to be on the board ..."

3. Withdraws

Withdraws from discussion; daydreams; does something else; leaves the room.

Examples:

Arms folded, looking away, talking to others, reading his mail.

"Whatever you say, it couldn't matter less to me. Let's get on with it."

4. Seeks Recognition

Needs constant support and affirmation.

Example:

"Have I done it right? Is this what you wanted" Maybe you'd prefer this ..."

Function of Group Members Observation Sheet

(put initials of each member at the top of each column)

MEMBER'S FUNCTIONS										
TASK FUNCTIONS:										
Defines Problem										
Seeks Information										
Gives Information										
Seeks Opinions										
Gives Opinions										
Tests Feasibility										
GROUP BUILDING & RELATIONSHIP FUNCTIONS										
Coordinating										
Mediating-Harmonizing										
Orienting-Facilitating										
Supporting-Encouraging										
Following										
INDIVIDUAL FUNCTIONS										
Blocking										
Digressing										
Withdraws										
Seeks Recognition										

Task and relationship roles are so crucial to group effectiveness that you might plan a series of related analyses to help members increase their understanding and expand their ability to put them into practice.

Distribute the task and relationship roles information (including the observation sheet) to members and request that they read it in preparation for the next meeting. Build time into the agenda to make a brief presentation of the roles, encouraging people to question and clarify their understandings. Facilitate a discussion of the value of enhancing these roles.

Break into two groups, assigning an observer (or two) for each. The observer writes each person's name at the top of the sheet. Ask one group to focus on practising task roles and the other to focus on practising relationship roles.

The question for discussion might be: "What things might we do as a group over our next four meetings to increase our ability to practise these roles?"

Give the group 8 - 10 minutes to discuss the question. The observer sits where she can see all members of the group and checks off functions (roles) that they contribute during the discussion. It is especially helpful if the observer records specific comments or actions.

At the conclusion of the discussion the observer gives feedback to the group about the ways in which they demonstrated either the task or relationship roles.

You might want to have each group listen to the feedback of the other. Share in the larger group the key discussion findings and suggestions.

Then, or at a subsequent meeting, have the groups switch focus, assign a new observer and select another question(s) for discussion.

Whenever you use observers, allow sufficient time for feedback to the group. Members will find the section on Feedback helpful here.

REFERENCES

1. Dimock, H.G., *Groups: Leadership and Development.* San Diego, CA: University Associates, 1987.

CHAPTER THREE
LEARNING MORE ABOUT GROUPS

There are many dimensions of group work worthy of study. To enhance your skill as a group member, practise observing real groups in action using the tools that follow.

VERBAL PARTICIPATION

Communication networks are easy to observe in groups and can provide insight into the interpersonal dynamics of the group and its potential for success. To do this yourself, represent everyone in your group as a dot. Place their initials or name beside the dot. Carefully observe who speaks to whom. If the person initiates the conversation, place a line with an arrow pointing in the direction of the communication. If the response is directed to a specific person, indicate that too. You'll want to record only short snippets of communication - perhaps no longer than five minutes. If you repeat the exercise three or four times throughout the meeting you will see patterns emerge.

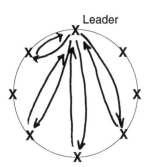

Leader

See how the leader initiates all discussion. It's a bit like watching a tennis match. The leader could break this cycle by posing a question to the whole group or diverting eye contact with the respondent. A member could add her comments unsolicited.

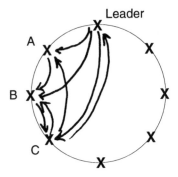

See how unbalanced discussion is at this meeting? A clique involving A, B and C exists. The leader directs comments to the clique, virtually ignoring other members. In the period observed, four people were not addressed, nor did they speak. Note the significance of position around the table to the ease with which cliques operate. When cliques dominate action, full participation is compromised.

Early in the group's development, most discussion is dialogue between the leader and one or other member of the group. Often when group members speak, they deliver a monologue to no one in particular. Later, alliances build that extend beyond the leader so that one person consistently supports and directs conversation to another. Patterns of communication emerge. Cliques may form and side conversations may occur that exclude segments of the group. Allies tend to sit together, supporting one another, even if the idea expressed is not sound. The silent person or the person who operates outside of group rules (person who dominates, person who expresses divergent views, person who uses vulgar language) may be excluded.

In a still later situation, communication is fully shared. People listen to the comments of others, responding to their intent. The leader is a group member who can participate fully but does not direct the flow of discussion. The open nature of the communication pattern invites everyone to get involved.

The Silent Member

The role of the leader is to encourage balanced participation throughout the whole group. He needs to actively seek out the opinions and ideas of silent members by:

❖ looking for cues that the silent members might wish to contribute (moving forward in chair, establishing eye contact, sharp intake of breath, responsiveness to a point or idea)

❖ asking the person directly to repeat a comment heard in a smaller group discussion or in one-to-one dialogue

❖ asking for information/opinion in an area where you know the person has expertise

❖ suggesting the group break into pairs to discuss a "hot topic" so that less confident people can contribute

❖ checking with a quiet member in a non-threatening way at a break to determine why he is silent

❖ smiling, nodding and making eye contact while asking for other opinions

❖ accepting that some people will participate less often than others.

Managing a Clique

To manage cliques and side conversations, the leader may:

❖ position himself to make side conversation difficult - beside or between group members

❖ identify the benefits of involving everyone in discussion, the value of all group members and the impact of exclusion

- ❖ ask members of the clique to share comments with the full group

- ❖ establish or refer to ground rules that promote participation by all

- ❖ deliberately mix small trios or pairs to promote wider discussion

POWER AND INFLUENCE

Another fascinating dimension of group dynamics is the study of power and influence. Even when all group members contribute to the discussion, some people's ideas and opinions appear to be more readily accepted. These include the person who:

IS DESIGNATED AS LEADER OR CHAIRPERSON

Leaders rarely appreciate the impact their words have on a group simply because they are the leader. An off-hand remark or casual suggestion can be taken as a directive. A wise chairperson does not preclude discussion by offering comments or advice without careful consideration of the consequences.

HAS STATUS IN ANOTHER ARENA LIKE

THE COMPANY LEADER

> The presence of the "boss" in a group dramatically alters the group dynamic, even if the boss is an enlightened and participative employer. Members may be reluctant to express true feelings if someone with power to hire and fire is in the room. Mixing a group will limit the frank nature of discussion, but may help to build a team if the leaders are prepared to listen without rebuke.

A person's profession may impact negatively on the message delivered. We are sometimes suspicious of these people and their opinions even if their views are well-documented.

CERTAIN PROFESSIONS (LAWYER, DOCTOR, PROFESSOR, PROFESSIONAL ATHLETE, ACTOR)

Expertise in one field may suggest to some competence in another when no such competence is evident. An actor may be declared a spokesperson for a group because he has recognition and status, but little background on the issue.

IS HIGHLY ARTICULATE

People who speak well, with passion and polish are listened to, even if their comments lack substance. Conversely, people who speak English poorly are discounted, even if their input is valid.

HAS PROVIDED SOUND DIRECTION IN THE PAST

People return to the same sources for help when faced with problems. An established leader will be consulted even if she is out of touch with the issue.

The role of the facilitator is to influence the group to listen to all points of view and not to dismiss someone who has a valid point. The leader can help by observing cues that suggest someone's opinion is negated:

- interrupting, talking over the idea as it is presented
- rolling of eyes (suggesting "here he goes again")
- making faces that suggest displeasure
- turning his back to speaker
- engaging in side conversation
- offering a suggestion as if the other never spoke.

What can the facilitator do to encourage the person with little influence to speak up and be heard? Try the following:

- ❖ model active listening skills, attentiveness, politeness

- ❖ let a person with language difficulties complete his thoughts without interruption

- ❖ re-phrase views of those less articulate to give them more weight

- ❖ compliment efforts to speak up - nod encouragement, give verbal recognition by name "What I especially liked about Jean's idea ..."

- ❖ make explicit group norms (rules) and expectations about valuing all comments

- ❖ be sure the new member is introduced into the group and her skills acknowledged "I believe Jean will be a great help to this group because of her skill in leadership development"

- ❖ ask others to summarize the viewpoint of a less powerful group member.

DECISION MAKING PROCESS

The purpose of all groups is to accomplish an agreed upon task. To do so decisions must be made. Observing how decisions are made can suggest needed improvements in the group process.

DOMINANT MEMBERS

Do one or two people assume they speak for the whole group when decisions are proposed? How can we slow the process down to be sure there is widespread agreement to proposals? Here are five techniques that may be helpful:

1. Ask for different perspectives on issues raised

For example, "Barb has raised this point. Who would propose a counterpoint?"

Point-counterpoint is a useful technique to ensure full exploration of solutions. The counterpoint is taking the opposite position and arguing for it.

> Example:
>
> Barb suggests we all make craft items for sale at the church bazaar, hoping to raise $600.00.
>
> Helen's counterpoint: If each person in the group contributes $30.00, we can raise the same amount without the effort. People are too busy to spend time making craft items.
>
> This counterpoint might lead to a third option whereby those people who like making crafts do so for the bazaar while those who prefer not to donate $30.00.

2. The Black Hat Approach

Edward DeBono [1], in his book *Six Thinking Hats,* has suggested a similar technique. He suggests that someone be assigned a "black hat" or devil's advocate position. That person's job in a group is to introduce an alternate way of solving the problem or asking questions that stretch the group's way of looking at things. As competence in using this technique increases, the chair can ask for "black hats". The approach does give someone permission to think critically and separates the person from the position. A sensitive chairperson would rotate the black hat to ensure that no one person is seen as consistently negative.

3. SUMMARIZE THE DECISION, ASK THE GROUP'S REACTION AND SUPPORT.

Example:

"Am I correct that we are proposing that everyone will sell raffle tickets? Do I have agreement for that? I'm noticing some shaking of heads."

4. INVITE FURTHER DISCUSSION.

Examples:

"Let's explore this a bit further."

"We have a proposal on the table. Are there other thoughts?"

5. CALL FOR A STRAW VOTE, A SHOW OF HANDS.

If there is still disagreement, ask for objections. Invite the person who offered a solution to respond to the suggestions.

A straw vote suggests the sense of the group but does not carry the sting of being out-voted in a group. Whenever possible, objections should be heard and dealt with to the satisfaction of the entire group. Votes with winners and losers weaken the solidarity and cohesiveness of the group. If time does not permit full discussion of an issue, efforts must be directed to bring the person who lost the vote back into the group as a full member.

EXPLORING ALL THE OPTIONS

Are decisions made prematurely, without exploring all the necessary background information? Ineffective problem solving often results when favoured tried and true solutions are applied to novel situations.

Nothing is more dangerous than an idea when it's the only one you have.   *- Emile Chartier*

The wise facilitator helps the group put in place processes and procedures that improve the decision-making and problem-solving abilities of that group.

GROUP ATMOSPHERE

Groups seem to flourish in an atmosphere of safety and mutual respect. When the climate is one of suspicion and mistrust, productivity is lessened. Shifts in the climate are significant. The facilitator must be able to diagnose current climate conditions within the group and between specific group members so that he can intervene to restore balance as quickly as possible.

❖ What is the feeling inside this group?

❖ Is it warm, friendly, accepting of new ideas or guarded and hostile?

❖ Are differences valued or merely tolerated?

❖ How are members controlled? (ridicule, exclusion, sarcasm, avoidance)

GROUP NORMS

All groups have rules for doing things that are accepted by the group as the "right" way to behave. Sometimes these rules are stated, for example, we will keep minutes. Often the rules are unexpressed and must be learned by the newcomer if he wants to become part of the group. A frank discussion of group norms will assist the group in the forming stages to determine how it will operate and may reduce conflicts that often surface. Chapter Eight looks at these stages of group development.

There are many unstated rules that determine how the group will function. Selecting out those that will assist the group to work together more effectively and lead to achievement of group goals should be encouraged.

EXAMPLES OF TOPICS FOR GROUP NORMS:

- how group members will interact
- how new members are oriented
- how leadership is determined
- how conflict is dealt with
- what happens if a member is absent or late
- how formally we will handle our business
- how much humour is allowed
- how members are disciplined

Ground Rules for a group might look like the following:

GROUND RULES

1. Everyone's opinion is important!

2. We will share leadership.

3. Conflict is an opportunity for growth and is viewed positively.

4. We will start on time and finish on time.

5. Smoking is permitted at the break only.

6. People who are absent must get in touch with another group member to catch up on group activities.

7. Only one person will talk at a time! No side conversations.

Creating Your Own Ground Rules

Help your group to identify the ways they want to work together. Early in the life of the group, it is helpful to determine the guidelines that will shape how the group will function.

Present the key concepts about group norms:

- All groups have rules for doing things that are supported by the group as "proper and correct".

- By making clear our expectations, group members will feel more confident and work will proceed more smoothly.

- Propose the following questions for discussion:

  - What do you believe is important when people come together as a group?

  - What advice do you have for members of the group to make you feel more comfortable to participate?

  - What guidelines would you suggest for this group in order to help us work more effectively?

Allow about half an hour to discuss in groups of four, recording information to be later shared in a full group discussion.

- Prepare a list of ground rules that is posted whenever the group meets. You will discover that group members will "police" one another whenever the rules are broken.

THE VALUE OF LISTENING

In his best seller *The 7 Habits of Highly Effective People*[2] ,Covey suggests that one habit worth cultivating is "Seek First to Understand ... Then to be Understood". This is good advice for the serious student of group improvement.

We are often so busy making ourselves understood that we fail to take the time to understand and appreciate the thoughts and feelings of others. We listen only to prepare our response, not to truly understand.

Covey claims we need a paradigm shift - focusing more time and effort on listening rather than talking. He proposes we engage in "empathetic listening". This is listening with your ears, head and heart. You are trying to get inside the other person's frame of reference to see the problem or issue as he does himself. You put yourself totally in his shoes. No thought or rebuttal, argument or even response demonstrates a clear investment in that person's point of view.

Contrast this with our usual listening style. We may drift in and out of attention, practise "selective listening", tune into issues that we believe are important or take a mental vacation when the issues seem less critical to our own well-being.

On the other hand, we may be practising "defensive listening". When we feel attacked we are busy protecting ourselves from your criticism. We build walls of "ya, buts", "if you only knew thats" and "not me, you can't say that to me". The speaker finds his communication hits the wall we have hastily constructed. Still trying to make his point, the speaker presses his comments more forcefully. Again, we react negatively.

How much better if we could drop the wall and instead construct a screen. Protected from heat, the criticism can pass through the screen, while we examine what has been said. We can accept or reject the comments, but the speaker knows he has been heard. The ranting and raving can stop.

BRUSH UP YOUR LISTENING SKILLS

Many people believe they are good listeners but in fact, they are not. When people are actively listening, pulse and blood pressure rates go up, muscles tense and there is a genuine sense of effort. Listening is not a passive act.

> *"We listen at about 25% of our potential, which means we ignore, forget, distort or misunderstand 75% of what we hear"*[3]

Many of the special problems in communicating sensitive or emotional material result from the assumption that we have understood what has been said. Effective listeners confirm their understanding by:

- reflecting back to the speaker what they heard, using their own words
- asking clarifying questions
- requesting more information

MANY FACTORS CAN GET IN THE WAY OF EFFECTIVE LISTENING

❖ preoccupation with other issues that overshadow the effort of listening

Example:

You left a sick child at home and your car is in the shop needing expensive repairs. As a result you can't concentrate on the lecture about promptness delivered by your committee chair.

❖ a strong response to the way a message is delivered

Example:

The person is standing face to face with you, speaking loudly, very close to your body and jabbing her finger at you.

❖ an emotional reaction to the content of the message. Certain "red flag" words may grab your attention and prevent your following the message.

Example:

"Well little lady, I just wouldn't worry about that if I were you!"

❖ language and cultural differences in presentation, use of words, personal space, timing

Example:

"Where's your pocketbook?" (American for purse or handbag, in Canada, a paperback book).

❖ the past performance of the speaker (for example, the person who is always negative is sometimes dismissed, even when he has a good point to offer).

❖ hearing or speech patterns or defects.

Example:

"Here's what I have in mind, you know."

❖ distractions while the message is delivered, noise, other pre-existing issues can deflect attention from the issue at hand.

Example:

A committee member leaves the room as you are making your presentation. All eyes are on her, no one is listening to you.

❖ lack of familiarity with the subject can encourage the listener to take a mental vacation.

Example:

"You add the override function to your basic energy packet creating multiple options for the sound system array. Of course, you'll need a supplementary speaker with stereophonic caps."

❖ a sense of personal threat, when you or an idea of yours are being criticized.

Example:

"Your report is completely unsatisfactory. What I had in mind was a much broader look at community development issues."

GOOD LISTENING IS FACILITATED WHEN:

• eye contact is maintained

• sentences are short and language is simple

• people listen for meaning behind the words

• verbal and non-verbal messages are the same

• the pace of information is slow with frequent pauses

• there is an opportunity to confirm what was understood

Using Questions to Facilitate Group Activity

A member can influence the effectiveness of the group or committee by using clarifying and questioning techniques.

When trying to gather information about an issue or concern, the following techniques may help you clarify what is meant or may encourage the group to think more carefully about what has been said.

Reflection:

This is a mirroring technique in which the listener plays back to the speaker the feelings and thoughts he believes are being expressed. It can be an extremely powerful technique for affirming that the person has been understood. Remember to use your own words, not those of the speaker.

Example 1:

Sally: "I just hate coming to these meetings."

John: "You don't like to come to our meetings because you find them so stressful." (note the listener has interpreted what he thought was the reason behind the feelings)

Sally: "No, I have to miss my bridge night when I come here."

Example 2:

Ed: "I'd like to get rid of that whole committee."

Jan: "You don't feel that group is doing a good job?"

Ed: "That's right! They never make a decision - just pass work over to us. We get dumped on all the time."

Jan: "You feel we are overworked while they slack-off?"

Ed: "Slack-off may be a bit strong. They do have a lot of work to do. I just wish they would include us more often in their planning. I guess it's the surprises that really upset me." (The real problem is identified - being hit with extra work unexpectedly. The committee can now devise some strategies to lessen the impact of unplanned work).

A Reflection Exercise

Carl Rogers, the noted therapist, has suggested the following exercise to reduce conflict and build understanding using the reflecting technique.

1. Identify a controversial topic for your group. Post it on a piece of flipchart paper.

2. Invite everyone to comment on the topic. Before a person adds a comment, however, she must repeat the comment of the person who spoke before her. They must use their own words to **reflect** both feeling and content.

3. Be sure everyone has a turn to both speak and reflect.

4. Have the full group discuss the learnings from this exercise.

5. You may want to encourage group members to talk about when this technique might best be used. A group of six to eight will take fifteen minutes to complete this exercise.

Practising the Reflection Techniques

Learning to reflect both the content of another's remark plus the feeling behind the words requires carefully honed listening skills. The benefits are many:

- ❖ the speaker knows his concerns have been heard

- ❖ the speaker is encouraged to explore his feelings and thoughts more thoroughly

- ❖ the listener can often determine the real problem clouded by intense emotion.

Two problems exist. The first is learning to reflect feelings without sounding like a parrot. When the words of the speaker are repeated verbatim, there is no evidence of understanding, just evidence that the words were repeated.

Example:

"I'm so disappointed at the results of our fundraising drive."

Parroting: "You are so disappointed at the results of our fundraising drive?"

Reflecting: "You feel we made a lot less than you expected?" "You feel we made less than we need to serve our clients well?"

In a parroted conversation, the speaker feels manipulated, not genuinely communicated with. Herein lies the second problem. Over-use of the technique makes the speaker feel like a tennis player in a game for one. Use the reflecting technique when:

- ◆ there is intense emotion
- ◆ you're uncertain about the real issue behind the emotion
- ◆ the speaker has not clearly communicated the issue.

Open Ended Questions:
Introduce questions that solicit discussion rather than a yes or no answer (if you are looking for more information).

Example:

"Let's talk about this issue. What are the important considerations we want to address?"

Closed Questions:
The speaker wants little discussion, simply a statement of fact. These are sometimes referred to as direct questions.

Example:

"How many visitors came to the Museum last year?"

Qualification of Wants and Feelings:
This technique is used to determine what the other person wants in a conflict situation.

Examples:

"What would bring this to a satisfactory conclusion in your opinion?"

"What would you like to see happen now?"

"How can I help you feel better about this?"

Asking for Feedback:
This technique is used to request a response to your own suggestions about how a situation is to be handled. The trick here is to really listen to the response and try not to be defensive of your own position.

Examples:

"What would you like to see me do differently in this situation?"
"What is your response to this proposal?"

"What additional changes do you need in our agreement?"

SILENCE:
Silence can be an important tool to slow the process down, to gain perspective, to invite response. Don't be afraid of silence or feel uncomfortable with it. If you feel very uneasy, try to use the silence to prepare a summary. "Here's what I've heard you say so far..."

Moving From Closed Questions to Open Ended Questions - An Exercise

The object of this exercise is to practise asking open ended questions. Working in pairs, start by changing the following questions from closed to open ended. Then continue your discussion using only open-ended questions. Whenever a closed question is asked, respond with "closed" and refuse to answer. This practice enhances listening as well as questioning skills.

1. What is your name?

2. Where do you live?

3. How many children do you have?

4. What kind of work do you do?

5. Do you have any hobbies?

6. Did you have a summer vacation?

7. Do you enjoy sports?

8. What book are you reading now?

9. Do you own a pet?

10. Have you ever been a volunteer?

This exercise will take about 20 minutes. Try to vary the format of questions to build your own "question bank".

Clarifying and Questioning Techniques
- An Observation Exercise

To build your own questioning skills, use this form to observe group discussion. Record examples of techniques used to gather information and clarify concerns. Many groups use only one or two techniques. The purpose of this practise is to encourage you to use as many as possible. Please be specific in your recordkeeping.

OBSERVER SHEET

TECHNIQUE	EXAMPLES OF WHAT WAS SAID AND WHEN
Reflection	
Open Ended Questions	
Closed Questions	
Qualification of Feelings	
Asking for Feedback	
Silence	

GUIDELINES FOR GIVING FEEDBACK

"Giving feedback is a verbal or non-verbal process through which a person communicates his or her perceptions and feelings about another person's behaviour." [4] In a group setting, feedback is ongoing. As members and leaders we want to ensure that the feedback is delivered in a helpful and supportive way so that the recipient can act on the information without feeling demeaned or attacked.

Giving feedback that may be critical or evaluative is a learned skill based on eight guidelines:

1. CONSIDER THE NEEDS OF OTHERS.

The purpose of feedback is growth for the other person, not to punish or belittle.

> Destructive: "That idea is really dumb. We can't get support for such a hare-brained notion."

> Constructive: "I feel uncomfortable with that proposal. My hope for this proposal would be that it include the participation of our ethnic communities."

2. DESCRIBE BEHAVIOUR OR CONTENT.

Do not label, blame or interpret. People are less likely to become defensive if feedback is free of blame or interpretation of the motive. Try to keep personality and intentions out of the conversation.

> Example:

> Interpreting: "I suspect your anger comes from your lack of experience."

> Labelling: "That's a very immature response. You'll see the issue more clearly when you are my age."

Rather, "I feel upset when you raise your voice in the group."

3. FOCUS ON BEHAVIOUR THAT CAN BE CHANGED OR IS PERTINENT TO THE CONCERNS OF THE GROUP.

Reflecting on personal style, habits or dress is not helpful. Criticizing someone's personal characteristics will not lead to a positive change but will lead instead to self-consciousness and withdrawal from the group.

Examples:

Ineffective: "Your grasp of English is limited, therefore I find myself not paying attention."

Effective: "Could you speak up a little please? I can't hear your comments as you are sitting at the far end of the table tonight."

4. BE SPECIFIC.

To provide insight, the recipient must clearly understand what behaviour is under discussion.

Generalized: "I liked your input tonight."

Specific: "Your recommendations on 'Safety in the Playground' were complete, well thought out and valuable to our deliberations."

5. ASK FOR PERMISSION TO GIVE FEEDBACK.

A speaker's wish to give feedback may be greater than the recipient's desire to receive it. Rather than drown someone with a flood of areas for improvement, select out one specific item for feedback. Ask for their agreement before you share the feedback. You may prefer to wait until the meeting is over if the information is personal, or if your own response is based on angry, unresolved feelings.

Examples:

"I'd like a chance to respond to that. May I tell you how that comment makes me feel?"

"Your presentation has really angered me. May I tell you why?"

6. GIVE FEEDBACK AS SOON AS POSSIBLE AFTER THE EVENT.

Most feedback can be delivered immediately after the event. It is not helpful to "store up" feedback to be dealt with at some future distant point. Behaviour can't be changed if no feedback is given. Furthermore, small irritants, left unattended, combine to create major communication barriers. Try to give focused feedback and then move on. Don't nag or refer back to previously delivered feedback.

7. ALLOW THE RECIPIENT THE RIGHT TO USE OR IGNORE THE FEEDBACK.

We usually expect that information delivered in a respectful and supportive manner will be acted upon, especially if the information suggests the discomfort of another. This may not be so. The recipient of the feedback must be granted the right to ignore the feedback once it has been delivered. He may perceive the feedback as an attempt to set external standards for his behaviour that are unacceptable to him. Imposing our own standards on the behaviour of others can foster resistance and resentment.

Example:

"It really upsets me when you speak to your mother like that. Children should respect their parents." (A standard is set by the speaker).

8. Express feelings directly.

Often people express their own opinion or give advice under the guise of describing their own feelings.

Example:

"I feel you should stop feeling sorry for yourself." (An opinion masquerading as feelings. This comment does not help anyone change behaviour).

Instead: "I feel so frustrated when you don't return my phone calls. "Am I not important to you?" Here frustration is the genuine feeling. See how the speaker interprets failure to return phone calls.

REFERENCES

1. De Bono, Edward, *Six Thinking Hats,* Penguin Books, 1985
2. Stephen Covey, *The 7 Habits of Highly Effective People,* Simon & Schuster, 1989.
3. Diane Bone, *The Business of Listening, A Practical Guide to Effective Listening,* Crisp Publications, Menlo Park, California, 1988
4. Hanson, P.G., "Giving Feedback: An Interpersonal Skill", *The 1975 Annual Handbook for Group Facilitators,* 1975

Points to Consider When Giving Feedback

☐   Am I leaving the other person the freedom to reject or accept what I am saying?

☐   Am I open to the other person's views and feelings?

☐   Am I being considerate of the other's feelings?

☐   Is this the right time to give feedback?

☐   Will the other person get angry?

☐   Can I accept this anger?

☐   What is the climate in our relationship - warm or hostile? Is it helpful or hindering?

☐   Am I honestly trying to be helpful to the other person?

☐   Do I have other motives?

Points to Consider When Receiving Feedback

☐   Am I listening closely when someone is presenting feedback and not making excuses for the behaviour in question?

☐   Am I giving hints that I am ready and willing to receive feedback?

☐   Am I ignoring the feedback, thus shutting off any other attempts to help me?

☐   Can I sort out the motives the other person may have and still be able to hear the positive contribution this person can make?

☐   Am I receiving non-verbal gestures, etc., that may be feedback?

☐   Am I being honest with myself when judging feedback presented to me, event when it may be presented with hostility, or lack of tact, etc.

☐   Am I resisting because I don't want to change my present way of behaviour?

☐   Am I willing to consider that I cannot grow unless I am open to constructive feedback and can profit from it?

Adapted from an article by Hanson, P.G. "Giving Feedback: An Interpersonal Skill", in J.E. Jones and J.W. Pfieffer 1975 Annual Handbook for Group Facilitators.

Practising the Giving of Feedback

After reviewing the *Guidelines for Giving Feedback*, spend a few minutes reviewing a situation where you had a heated exchange of feedback. Perhaps it was not constructive and helpful.

Replay the event, exploring alternate responses to comments made. Consult *Points to Consider When Giving Feedback* to help you. What did you really feel? How might you approach the same situation today? Consider meeting with the individual to review the exchange and to clarify your feelings.

Plan for the Future

Before you enter another situation that may be tense, consider what your real feelings are. Plan how you will deliver the required feedback. Are you following the guidelines? Do any comments label or demean? What changes can you make to lessen the defensiveness and allow the feedback to be heard?

CHAPTER FOUR

DECISION-MAKING IN GROUPS

TYPES OF DECISIONS

Much of the work of groups involves making decisions. How do we ensure that decisions made are sound, well-considered and will gain the acceptance of all members?

In times of emergency, when fast action is required, a COMMAND decision may be necessary. The leader of the group takes action, often without consultation. For example, an article appears in the press about your agency. When the President receives a call from a local TV station, he responds without clearing his comments with the Board or the Executive Director. If the President is well informed about the issue involved, the comments will probably be appropriate. Interaction with the press needs freedom to act independently - the approval of the Board is of less importance in this situation. If an individual or group uses the COMMAND mode too often, the membership feels shut out of decision-making, especially around issues that affect them. This builds resistance and reluctance to support initiatives even if they are wisely constructed. The command mode should be used only when time is short or if the need for commitment by others is small.

When the buy-in and support of the members is more important, leadership may adopt a CONSULTATIVE approach. For example, the Board is considering a change in the structure of your organization. It sends letters to all five standing committees inviting their input in the making of the decision. Representatives of membership are also consulted about their positions on the issue. The Board, having gathered all the opinions, weighs the merits of each position and makes a decision about how restructuring will occur. Some people may not feel very satisfied with the outcome of the consultation if their view is not reflected in the final decision, but their opinion will have been heard. This process is very much slower than the command decision.

Most participative management operates on a consultative basis. A relatively small group of people make decisions after assembling the data and evaluating the evidence. Those who feel that their opinion should be adopted if it is sought, miss the point of this approach. A complex tangle of variables determine the final decision:

- view of the majority
- perceived benefit of proposals vs. perceived losses
- size of resistance and its location
- other barriers to implementation
- external forces that press for change

To reach a sound decision, all of these factors and more must be put into the mix. A single viewpoint becomes less compelling given the larger context.

A third type of decision-making that is spreading in use is that of CONSENSUS building. In this type of decision, buy-in is critical and participants are prepared to invest considerable time to see that all parties can support the final decision. For example, in building a community collaboration, it is essential that all members feel fully satisfied with the mission of the group. To vote on the mission, declaring support for a majority position, creates winners and losers in the assembly of the organizations. No group would agree to provide funding and human resources to a mission it could not wholeheartedly support.

Reaching consensus does not mean total agreement but rather comfort with the position. The question posed is "Can you live with this statement?", not "Are you in complete agreement with it?"

Reaching consensus depends on trust - the belief that other members of the group are as anxious to see your needs met as they are to having their own requirements achieved. Often when consensus is required, the group may come with very different views, strongly felt and deeply rooted in a past history of conflict or perceived wrong doing. Examples include bitter negotiations between labour unions and management, warring sides in a territorial dispute, or even individuals with very different agendas for a single organization. The challenge of building trust under these circumstances is enormous. However, to move forward to resolution, it is an essential ingredient of success. Fortunately, the work we do in consensus decision-making rarely results in such fixed positions.

GAINING CONSENSUS FOR DECISIONS

1. BUILD TRUST AND RAPPORT AMONGST THE GROUP

Allow time for the group members to get to know each other and you. Spend time listening to their backgrounds, what they bring and are willing to share with the group. Acknowledge all contributions as potentially useful and valid. Support early efforts to decide how the group will work together. Discover what each member needs to feel included in the group.

2. GET AGREEMENT ON THE PURPOSE AND VALUE OF THE DECISION

Build a mutually acceptable purpose. Create a common vision.

3. BRAINSTORM A LIST OF POSSIBLE METHODS

to accomplish the goal of the decision. No evaluation allowed. No discussion allowed. Encourage the group to be as far out as possible.

4. ELIMINATE THE TRULY UNACCEPTABLE OPTIONS

in full group discussion. Everyone must support the elimination of a response before it is removed. Priorize the remaining solutions. You may be left with two or three that are popular.

5. IDENTIFY CONSEQUENCES OF THE ACCEPTABLE ALTERNATIVES

You may want to break into small groups in which the consequences are fully explored. Groups report back and again an effort is made to select a single alternative that has the support of everyone.

6. NAME THE BARRIERS THAT MAKE IT UNCOMFORTABLE

for the committee members to agree with one or the other approach. What is getting in the way of our coming to agreement? Each member should identify what it is she is unhappy about taking ownership for her own feelings or comments. For example, "I hesitate to support that approach because I feel it is too aggressive." If people are unwilling to do this in front of the whole group have them work in twos or submit a written comment.

7. IDENTIFY WHAT CHANGES YOU NEED

to make it acceptable for you. The golden question is often, "How must I change this initiative to win your support?" An example might be, "I could buy this approach if only one volunteer made the visit when asking for funds." Often to gain acceptance you will need to make several small changes.

8. DECIDE

either to make the requested changes, to review another alternative to see if agreement can be more easily reached or WALK AWAY.

9. DEVELOP COMMITMENTS AND EXPECTATIONS

that are clearly defined, well thought out and realistic. Get agreement on how and when results are to be reported.

THE PHASES OF DECISION-MAKING

Like planning, decision-making is made up of four phases.

PREPARATION PHASE

1. Clarification of purpose and plan.

2. Introduction of all group members with an opportunity to identify what each group member brings to the discussion.

3. Warm up activity that illustrates how group will work together. Establishes supportive, comfortable climate. Research suggests that groups gain skill in decision-making with practise as a group.

4. Presentation of the item for discussion - clarification, questions, data gathering.

EXPANSION PHASE

1. Generating a large number of possible solutions/ courses of action - no evaluation at this point.

CONTRACTION PHASE

1. Clarify what is meant by each option.

2. Eliminate completely unworkable suggestions.

3. Identify consequences of each option.

4. Priorize using criteria for acceptance that have been mutually developed.

5. Select a course of action.

COOL DOWN PHASE

1. Gain commitment for approach.

2. Plan objectives, action steps, budget.

3. Determine success measures - when and how project is to be evaluated.

4. Implement.

TECHNIQUES TO ENHANCE DECISION-MAKING

BRAINSTORMING

Most people are familiar with the technique of **brainstorming**, used during the expansion phase of decision-making. Here are a few pointers for generating a large number of new ideas.

❖ Present the problem statement. Keep the issue as simple and as focused as possible.

❖ Outline the rules of brainstorming:

  ◆ Purpose: to generate as many ideas as possible
  ◆ No criticism or evaluation
  ◆ Build on the ideas/work of others
  ◆ Quantity is more important than quality
  ◆ Free association is encouraged
  ◆ All WILD ideas are welcome
  ◆ No commenting or suggestions

❖ Consider a warm-up that involves brainstorming. Research indicates that idea generation increases with practise.

❖ Continue after the first wave of enthusiasm. The leader should feel free to add to the list.

❖ Create a mechanism to capture good ideas after the session. Many creative ideas are generated after some thought.

❖ When all ideas have been contributed, move on to the evaluative phrase.

When faced with a very complex problem or issue, consider using the Force Field Analysis technique designed by Kurt Lewin [1]. The concept underlying this technique is that at any given time, countervailing forces are at work keeping a particular situation in place. To make a change happen, you must:

Strengthen the forces that support the change (DRIVING FORCES)

Reduce or eliminate forces that work against the change happening (RESTRAINING FORCES)

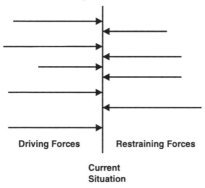

Driving Forces | Restraining Forces

Current Situation

Current situation - We have been unable to recruit any new committee members.

Desired state - We want a full slate of active, well-prepared committee members.

Gail attended a seminar on recruiting

No organized recruitment plan

3 members have left who are not yet replaced

Our fabulous chairperson resigned

Our meetings are held in the afternoons when few people are available

Our reputation is great in the community

No orientation offered

We are achieving good results with our work. People enjoy the meetings

No one has time to recruit

Driving Forces | **Restraining Forces**

Current Situation

1. A small group of 8-10 are assembled to analyze the problem.

2. A desired state or condition is identified.

3. What forces will help us achieve our desired state? (These are DRIVING forces).

4. What forces may block achievement of our desired state? (RESTRAINING forces).

5. After forces have been identified, we explore strategies to:

+ strengthen DRIVING FORCES
  eg. Gail has attended a recruiting seminar. Could she teach several of us how to recruit?

+ remove or reduce RESTRAINING FORCES
  eg. would we consider changing our meeting time to make it more attractive to new recruits?
  eg. would we develop an orientation program?

+ Some forces will not be changeable.
  eg. The chairperson has resigned. Three members have left.

+ Some forces can move from restraining to driving forces if action is taken.
  eg. No orientation can become a driving force if it is well-planned and implemented.

6. Select strategies for action that will be most likely to bring about the desired change.

Pairs, trios, small groups - there are a variety of ways in which people can relate to each other. Some grouping are better than others for achieving different outcomes. In general, the chart below sets out effective (+) and ineffective (-) groupings for different objectives [2].

	Alone	Pair	Trio	Group 5-8	Total Group
Reducing Anxiety	+	+	++	+	—
Generating Ideas	—	—	+	++	+
Clarifying Ideas	+	+	++	++	—
Identifying Pros & Cons	+	+	++	++	—
Identifying Consequences	+	+	++	++	++
Making Decisions that will affect the group	—	—	—	++	++
Plan details	++	++	+	—	—
Practise skills used in one-to-one situations	—	++	++	+	—
Practice skills used in groups	—	—	+	++	++

Reports and Presentations

One of the potentially deadly segments of any meeting is the reporting of past action. Keep discussion of past events to a minimum so that you can focus your efforts on future action. Meetings are not best suited to monologue-style information giving. Use the opportunity for dialogue and debate.

Presentations are often a part of data gathering that can enliven the group discussion. Several pointers to ensure success:

❖ make sure the presenter knows who the audience is and the purpose of the presentation

❖ limit questions during the presentation to points of clarification to keeps the full group's attention

❖ pre-circulate questions that will be addressed after the presentation, to sharpen listening skills. Develop the questions with the help of the presenter, if possible. Here are some useful sample questions:

  ♦ what are the key concepts of this presentation?

  ♦ what is the impact of the information for our group?

  ♦ how might we respond to the situation described?

❖ encourage note taking which may be referred to in later discussion

Dealing With Feelings

When lively debate is encouraged, feelings and friction are not far behind. Rather than ignore or minimize feelings, a skilled facilitator must acknowledge and work with them to move the group forward. Kayser[3] suggests that "few things in the facilitator's tool kit are more important that an understanding of this simple sequence of group behaviour: feelings, facts, solutions." Each element must be handled before dealing with the next.

For many new facilitators, feelings are scary. They do cloud reason and good judgment. Lurking in the back of the facilitator's mind is the concern that talking about feelings will open a Pandora's box that will cause the group to "lose control". Exploring feelings, however, can be a release rather than a block.

SURVIVAL STRATEGIES

1. STAY COOL

Don't allow yourself to be swept into an emotional response. If you are facilitating, you need to concentrate on listening, understanding and helping others express their feelings. How do you indicate acceptance without taking sides?

- nodding your head, looking thoughtful

- reflecting what you've heard

- thanking the person for her input

- listening intently without interruption or impatience

- responding in a neutral tone "I hear that you feel very strongly about this."

2. LISTEN FOR UNDERSTANDING, NOT TO EVALUATE

Your task is to accurately hear out what the other group member is saying. You need to employ a "third ear" that hears beyond the words to the intent of what is said. Put yourself as much as possible in the shoes of the other person. This is not the time to point out why you feel her reaction is unwarranted or inappropriate. You'll want to be very sure that you have confirmed with the speaker the intent of the message. Ask for clarification or further detail. If possible, probe to discover the concern that is the basis for the feeling. Press for further clarification using questions or comments like: "Tell me how you feel...", "Uh huh...", "Is there a specific issue that worries (angers, frightens) you?"

3. WATCH FOR NON-VERBAL CUES

Non-verbal body language indicates emotions just below the surface. You'll want to invite the group member to bring forward these feelings. Cues to note include:

- the finger pointed during a comment

- the rigid body posture

- a turn from the group

- the rolling of the eyes

Model a careful separation of ideas from individuals. The expression of feelings is not an opportunity to attack another participant, but rather a time to explore the response to an idea or a behaviour. Learning more as a group about giving helpful feedback is discussed in Chapter Three.

Be on the lookout for verbal indications of feelings too, the sharp tone of voice, words quickly and forcibly expressed, words delivered in slow, painful hesitation.

4. ACKNOWLEDGE THE EXPRESSION OF FEELINGS

This doesn't imply agreement, but simply acceptance that those feelings exist. Trying to divert people to move away from the feelings prematurely will not help them focus on the group goals.

5. PAUSE

Slow the action down so everyone can consider what has been said. This gives you a chance to take a deep breath and plan how you want to proceed. A moment or two of internal reflection gives weight to the feelings expressed, allowing people to pinpoint their own reactions and to regain composure.

6. Separate Personal Issues from Group Concerns

There is a decision point here that needs discussion. Some outbursts are not related to the work of the group, but reflect a personal agenda. You may choose to redirect the group to the purpose of the meeting after thanking the speaker for his comments. For example:

> *Vince, an invited guest, began his introductory remarks to the financial group with an angry attack on the client services policy of the organization. The finance group had no control over the policy that was the source of Vince's tension. The chair thanked Vince for his comments, promising to direct his concerns to the appropriate committee and urged him to continue his presentation.*

Notice that the chair did not consult others about their feelings around this issue. Nor did she explore alternative approaches to solving Vince's problem. She moved the group and Vince back to the stated purpose of his presentation.

Contrast that with the following example:

> *Angela's lips were compressed into a thin, hard line when Jacob announced the layoff proposal. "But promises were made..." she blurted out. Jacob sensed that Angela was not the only person who felt betrayed. "Maybe we need to talk more about this before final decisions are made."*

Jacob is acknowledging the intense feelings in the room. They need further exploration. They are derived from items under discussion by the group. Invite a further discussion of feelings if they are related to the work of the committee.

The most comfortable technique for exploring feelings is to have the group talk quietly together in pairs for three or four minutes before bringing the whole group together. This allows anonymity when negative or possibly critical feelings are shared. Ask each pair to identify their feelings and the concerns that they have. List all feelings and concerns on flipchart paper. Summarize the themes uncovered in the full group feelings. Often this will diffuse the tension felt. You can post the flipchart sheet, remembering to re-visit it when you reach the decision-making phase of your discussion.

A second approach is to pitch right in and deal with the specific concerns expressed. That might be very important in the above example because it concerns a breach of trust. Until trust is restored, no meaningful contribution will be made. Assign groups of four to determine how they would resolve the concerns expressed. Allow 15 to 20 minutes to discuss a variety of options in the small groups, asking people to return with a verbal report back. The facilitator checks back with those who raised the concerns to see if the issues are now satisfactorily resolved.

Return the group to the purpose, desired results and agenda. Working on feelings is hard work! Summarize the decisions or position of the group, praise the efforts made to work together and re-focus the group's attention on it's goals and objectives.

Encourage balanced participation by all group members. A good facilitator is often a traffic cop - urging reluctant participants to speak up, staying the dominant or aggressive members, establishing an order of speaking when several participants comment at the same time. To learn more about this function, see Chapter Nine.

COLLABORATIVE DECISION-MAKING

Building support starts very early in the life of a committee. A wise facilitator must find out what each participant needs to be successful. This is especially true in collaborating or with representatives of diverse groups who come together to work on a project of mutual interest.

Strong committees, like good teams, are built on mutual concern. When members of a committee are dissatisfied or uncomfortable with a position declared by the majority of that committee, estrangement takes place. It is worth the time spent to explore the source of concern and to make the necessary alterations to win full agreement. You must determine "what changes in this position must we make to gain your support?" Your efforts, if genuine, build commitment to the proposal and to the committee, even if full agreement is not possible. You are trying to adapt to the needs of the other person. Let's look at the following example of collaborative effort.

A community project was initiated for street youth. Six organizations agreed to sponsor the program. Each had very different reasons for involvement:

Public Health Department - concerned about preventing teen pregnancy, sexually transmitted diseases and drug abuse.

Businessmen's Association - concerned about street crime, shoplifting, community discomfort in visiting their stores when young people were loitering around their stores.

Council of Churches - felt many of these children had been physically and sexually abused and were lost souls. Wanted to give them a second chance.

Department of Education - wanted to provide a tutoring program for early high school dropouts so that some young people might consider re-entry into the school system.

Recreation Centre - believed that a sports and fitness program would develop positive self-esteem and a sense of mastery for young people. They might then volunteer as junior leaders in their facility.

A Food Bank - was alarmed by the increase in the number of young people coming regularly for food. Wanted to address the problem of street youth at its roots.

You can see that to build support for a single initiative, many diverse needs are brought to the table. How many are complementary? How many are compatible? The facilitator at the very first meeting might pose one or more of the following questions:

1. What needs do you hope to see addressed?

2. What results would indicate to you that this project was successful?

3. What is your wish for our work together?

The facilitator records the wishes of all around the table on a piece of flipchart paper.

As each session closes, the facilitator might return to the stated wishes to determine if they are still valid and if progress is being made towards their achievement.

FACILITATOR AS ROLE MODEL

Model responsible risk taking by:

* Sharing Leadership
* Asking for Feedback
* Acknowledging Resistance

The facilitator has a significant part to play as a role model. He gives permission to other group members to behave as he does. His willingness to share leadership indicates his confidence in other group members as it builds their skills. He celebrates their achievements, welcoming their emergence as future leaders.

In the same way, he is not afraid of feedback - viewing it as an opportunity for personal growth. He seeks it out as part of a performance check and during regular evaluation sessions. He might use a questionnaire to gather group feelings or might pose any one of the questions listed to determine group satisfaction. If he feels participants will be uncomfortable giving direct feedback, he provides opportunities to do so anonymously.

The facilitator accepts as natural, resistance to change. He does not cajole, belittle or ignore it. He encourages expressions of resistance, letting group members explore their feelings so they can be dealt with candidly.

PROMOTING GROUP DISCUSSION: HOW ARE WE DOING?

The purpose of this form is to encourage discussion of the functioning of our group. It can be used, one question at a time, with people writing in their comments anonymously or it can be filled in completely outside of the meeting and people asked to send in their forms for tabulation. Another option is to have the chair lead a discussion of any one of these questions.

REFERENCES

1. M.S. Spicer, Kurt Lewin's "Force Field Analysis" in 1973 *Annual Handbook for Group Facilitators*, Editors J.E. Jones & J.W. Pfieffer, San Diego, CA, University Associates.
2. Abbey-Livingston, Diane and Kelleher, David, *Managing for Learning in Organizations: The Fundamentals*, Government of Ontario, 1988
3. Kayser, Thomas A., *Mining Group Gold*, Pfeiffer & Company, 1990, p. 103

How Are We Doing?

1.   When I was asked to serve on this group, I understood my role was:
2.   I was asked to serve on this committee because:
3.   Before I joined the committee, I wish someone had told me:
4.   I would feel more effective as a committee member if:
5.   The major problem facing our committee is:
6.   What I like best about our committee meetings are:
7.   What I dislike most about our committee meetings are:
8.   To improve our committee I think we should:

CHAPTER FIVE
RESOLVING CONFLICT IN GROUPS

RESOLVING CONFLICT

Many of us have been raised to believe that conflict is unnatural, undesirable and just plain not nice. As a result, we try to avoid or ignore conflict when it surfaces. Sometimes it occurs in the group or between meetings, when you receive indignant phone calls about who did what to whom at the last meeting. Rather than explore the conflict, our approach in dealing with it is to wait, hoping it will "take care of itself". Only when it becomes completely unsupportable do we take action. The response then is often extreme because we have allowed the incident to fester, unchecked for a long time. We drop an atomic bomb on a situation that might be better handled by a fly swatter.

Three responses are common in dealing with conflict in a group:

ONE PARTY MUST LOSE

> There is a power struggle with one side insisting that it must be victorious. The negotiation takes on the air of armed combat. There is a bunker mentality. At the end, one segment of the group feels victimized and defeated. They don't agree with the decision reached, they just feel unable to keep up the struggle. Will they work on behalf of the initiative? Unlikely. Will they speak in its defense if there is opposition from outside of the committee? Less likely still. This is really a classic example of having won the battle but lost the war!

EVERYONE MUST COMPROMISE

> This means everyone can win a little but everyone must also lose a little. Everyone settles for less than full satisfaction. There is a general sense of unease about the solution but no one feels crushed. People around the

table will support a proposal achieved through compromise but they lack passion or fire. They are going through the motions, often without the commitment that is required to see proposals through the rough spots.

EVERYONE CAN WIN

In this scenario, there is a new approach to problem solving. Creative initiatives are sought out. It becomes apparent that the old tried and true solutions won't work in this case, so new directions and new connections are forged. Instead of people getting stuck with traditional demands, they set out on a different path to solve the problem. There is a synergy amongst opposing points of view that generates energy, commitment and new solutions. The participants move from conspirators trying to manipulate others to "see it their way" to people who listen, cooperate and co-create, breaking new ground.

Seen in this light, conflict becomes a potentially positive experience, an opportunity for growth and experimentation. When everyone knows that his concerns will be addressed and that all parties will invest in helping the others achieve satisfaction, there is no need to be defensive. You can concentrate on listening and thoughtful problem solving.

WHERE TO START?

As with so many other group activities, the start point is not what you say but rather what you hear. Put aside your own position and hear what the other person NEEDS. Often in a dispute we offer our solution to the problem as we see it, even before we fully understand the NEED that is unmet.

For example, a group is meeting to discuss how service could be improved at City Hall.

- ❖ One segment of the group feels that the only solution is more staff.

- ❖ Another feels the only solution is the purchase of expensive computer equipment.

- ❖ A third group feels that the level of service is more than adequate, thank you very much.

It is only after considerable fractious debate that the original need is revealed. A community group wants services to be available in French. It's clear that none of the three positions would automatically meet the need. Instead, time, money and personnel might have been deployed without the desired result, French-speaking staff who could deliver service to Francophone residents.

PRINCIPLES TO RESOLVE CONFLICT

SEPARATE THE NEED FROM YOUR PERSONAL SOLUTION.

Much of the heat in conflict comes from the desire to have your own solution implemented. When you step back to address the problem, there may be many other possible solutions that can emerge. One of the other solutions may meet the needs of the other party equally well. Try to keep yourself open to all the possibilities.

Because people feel uncomfortable with conflict, they react by seizing the first solution they can find, often an old familiar one, even if it doesn't quite fit. They ignore the inconsistencies and the disarticulations. That one response becomes their "position".

> **Position:** "We need to hire a staff person to keep our office open in the evening."

Need: In order to respond to volunteer trends, we want to keep the office open in the evenings.

Possible Solutions:

- Hire an additional person
- Rotate volunteers through evening hours
- Stagger the start of the day to allow current staff to cover evening hours twice a week
- Close every morning. Open office from 11:00 a.m. to 7:00 p.m. every day

FIND OUT WHAT THE OTHER PARTY WANTS

Ask what the other party wants to have happen, not in terms of a solution but an end result. In the above example, the end result or need is that the office remains open in the evening. Consider the following questions when trying to uncover what the other party wants:

1. What need are you trying to meet?

2. What end result would make you feel satisfied that we were on the right track?

3. What are your wishes for the result in this situation?

You may need to do some listening, probing and interpreting to get away from a fixed solution to the real need. Often there are several mini-problems blended into a larger issue, so working through them may be a bit like peeling layers of an onion. Make sure the solutions developed address the needs expressed.

Elaine Yarborough[1] shares an effective technique that helps when tempers flare and progress seems unattainable. Call a 30 minute recess, encouraging people to go off on their own to think through what they really NEED. Sitting by a lake, in a garden, by yourself over a cup of coffee, listening to your own internal voice without interruption or perceived threat can help you clear away confusion and determine need.

WORK TO RESOLVE THE CONCERNS OF THE OTHER PARTY

Put your own needs on hold and work hard to resolve the fears of the other party. What can you do to comfortably meet his requests? This does not mean that you give up valued holdings to achieve success. Then you will leave the conflict feeling resentful. Instead, look for genuine points of negotiation where neither of you feel you have capitulated.

In this situation it is often helpful to review those things on which you already agree. By creating a common vision, you establish a platform for shared beliefs and values. Arguments are often focused on methods and activities. You can honestly acknowledge your shared commitment to common goals. This builds respect and trust that is so important in negotiation. Tracing common beliefs helps you identify points of disagreement. Now you know what is specifically blocking resolution of this issue. Set to work on it!

WORK TO ELIMINATE BARRIERS TO RESOLUTION

Sometimes in a conflict situation, you feel uncomfortable even though you agree with the substance of the discussion. It's rather like being sold a vacuum cleaner at the door. It sounds like a good deal. You need a new vacuum. But you feel pressured, bull-dozed or uncertain.

Barriers can be raised that are both content and style issues. Is it the tone of speech or is it the presentation? Are you being pressured? Is the discussion layered with sarcasm? Try to identify what is getting in the way for resolution of this issue.

Any participant of a group should feel free to call a time-out, to encourage the other party to back off and give some carefully worded feedback about how she is feeling. (See Chapter Three on feedback).

Often the other participant is unaware of his presentation style but is caught up in the heat of the debate. When this is brought to consciousness, you can anticipate a change in behaviour.

This phase seeks to ensure that mutually agreed upon solutions are implemented as promised and in a timely fashion. The components of the action plan outline:

- task to be done
- indicators that it has been done satisfactorily
- person responsible for implementation
- date by which it will be done
- report back mechanism.

Each party in the dispute should sign the action plan and each shares responsibility to see that it is implemented as agreed. Some people prefer that a neutral party, for example, the chairperson, might supervise the implementation.

It's true that people respect what you inspect. If the issue is worth a fiery debate, it is worth keeping an eye on the progress towards implementing its resolution. If misunderstandings develop, move in immediately to pinpoint the problem so each party can take corrective action as required.

REFERENCES

1. Private conversation with Elaine Yarborough

SECTION B
THE ROLE OF THE GROUP LEADER

CHAPTER SIX
LEADERSHIP

A WORD ABOUT LEADERSHIP

What makes so many people hesitant or reluctant to chair a committee? Anticipated workload is obviously a major factor for those with busy schedules. Hesitance sometimes stems, however, from people's lack of confidence in their ability to lead a group effectively.

Unfortunately, organizations often persuade caring and capable people to chair boards and committees without providing them with the training they need to develop the necessary leadership skills.

The philosophical foundation of this book rests on the belief that all members share responsibility for the success of the group. In this section, however, we will address those areas of responsibility that are especially important for a chair or leader, whether that person is new or experienced.

> *He who would be a leader*
> *Let him be a bridge*
> *Building bridges to the light*
> *Is the purpose of life*
>
> *Ancient Oriental Writing*

Much has been written about leadership - qualities, characteristics, styles and the like. Reflecting on what would be most helpful for people in leadership positions, we want to share with you the thoughts of several writers whose insights have shaped our vision of leadership. We encourage you to add these resources to your personal library and revisit them regularly. Our hope is that you will find insights and understandings that will not only enhance your leadership potential but which will as well refresh and inspire you on a personal level.

Current literature describes personal and organizational leadership in terms of vision, values and the empowerment of others. The growing emphasis on ethics and ethical values reflects a trend in organizational development to be values-driven, with a clearly articulated code of values and beliefs.

Two publications that reflect this ethical approach and which readers will find especially inspiring are *The Leadership Challenge* by Kouzes and Posner [1] and *The 7 Habits of Highly Effective People* by Stephen Covey [2].

In a study of 500 senior and middle management executives leading their organizations to extraordinary accomplishments, Kouzes and Posner identified five leadership practices common to successful leaders and in these practices, ten behaviourial commitments. Their fundamental belief is that these practices and commitments are not magically inherited by a privileged few, but can be learned by anyone interested in enhancing leadership skills. Their research identified:

CHALLENGING THE PROCESS:
Leaders contribute most when they are pioneers and innovators who actively challenge the status quo. Their proactive commitments are to always search for opportunities, to recognize good ideas and to experiment and take risks.

INSPIRING A SHARED VISION:
Creating a vision and inspiring others to develop commitment are practices that build a shared dream, ignited and sustained by people's enthusiasm.

ENABLING OTHERS TO ACT:
Their research supports the fact that exemplary leaders consistently foster collaborative efforts as well as strengthen others in the group to make them feel capable and committed.

MODELLING THE WAY:

Leaders earn respect through the behaviours they demonstrate. Successful leaders practice what they preach and organize their activities by planning small wins that over time make a difference.

ENCOURAGING THE HEART:

Successful leaders recognize other's contributions and ensure that both individual and group accomplishments are celebrated widely.

Readers searching for inspiration and greater understanding will find *The Leadership Challenge* an exceptional resource.

For those leaders trying to use time effectively, to manage multiple demands and to nurture friendships, families, careers and themselves, *The 7 Habits of Highly Effective People* is invaluable.

Covey criticizes the standard self-help manuals and time management handbooks that offer techniques to make you more efficient and effective. He suggests that techniques are superficial and lack substance. He believes that success is based on your innermost values and beliefs and requires that you identify your personal mission statement and use that as your organizing principle.

Covey presents a paradigm containing seven habits. Three habits he labels the private victory, habits that build inner confidence and consciousness. The second three are public victory issues that relate to relationships. Covey speaks of dependence, moving to independence and then to the ultimate state of interdependence. He acknowledges the importance of reaching out beyond oneself to give life meaning and direction. The last habit, sharpening the saw, relates to the need for balance in the mental, physical, spiritual and emotional components of our nature.

An article in the *Harvard Business Review* by Kim and Mauborgne[3] titled "Parables of Leadership" identified five essential qualities and acts of leadership that define a leader. Through a series of parables the authors help readers understand that true leaders demonstrate:

- the ability to hear what is left unspoken
- humility
- commitment
- the value of looking at reality from many vantage points
- the ability to create an organization (group) that draws
- out the unique strengths of every member

These simple parables demonstrate the essence of leadership. They speak to the heart and offer helpful insights into human behaviour.

A different perspective is suggested by Marilyn MacKenzie in an article titled "Creative Followership" published in the Spring 1989 edition of *Voluntary Action Leadership*[4]. She notes that a great deal of attention has been lavished on leadership, its style, its development, its methods and its future.

The time has come to focus attention on the rest of the people in the group - the followers. She believes that the act of following is not passive and sheeplike but rather a challenging role that can at times be difficult.

To be a good follower one must be able to deal with confusion, ambiguity and uncertainty. Our understanding of teamwork suggests that followers have an equally important part to play in the creation and achievement of goals and objectives, in the accomplishment of tasks grand or small.

Traditional definitions of leadership make it clear that there is a contract, perhaps unstated but implied: This is my job - leader; This is your job - follower.

Consider turning to a more fruitful pursuit: "creative followership" and study the roles and responsibilities of a truly creative and committed follower.

THREE PRINCIPLES OF CREATIVE FOLLOWERSHIP:

1. A CREATIVE FOLLOWER PARTICIPATES WHOLEHEARTEDLY IN ALL PHASES OF THE ENTERPRISE. THIS MEANS:

- when serving on a committee, one attends meetings
- coming prepared to discuss issues that are on the agenda
- voicing concerns when one has them, not later to complain about the decision
- supporting decisions, not sabotaging them with "It wasn't my idea".

2. A CREATIVE FOLLOWER DISPLAYS A WILLINGNESS TO LISTEN TO REASON, OPEN TO NEW POSSIBILITIES.

The creative follower functions rather like an expensive camera with a wide angle and a zoom lens, to grasp both the big picture and the detailed local scene. It is important to understand which lens to look through to get the best shot - to function most effectively on behalf of the committee.

3. A CREATIVE FOLLOWER IS GENUINELY COMMITTED TO WORKING WITH THE GROUP TO DEVELOP SOLUTIONS, PLANS AND PROGRAMS.

Creative followers work with others, not because the boss is in charge, but because they value collective effort and together create a superior product.

Good followers are made, not born. Powerful tools shaping their emergence are: clearly written expectations; frequent feedback and encouragement and the presence of visible role models.

Everyone can have a hand in "birthing" creative followers. Their training is a shared responsibility. Everyone involved has the privilege and the obligation of training with GRACE - Guidance, Respect, Accountability, Creativity, Excellence.

❖ Followers need **guidance** not rules or smothering.

❖ Followers deserve **respect**.

❖ Followers are **accountable** and may need to be reminded that there are expectations and standards.

❖ Followers need to be encouraged to be **creative**, to be the best they can, not to do things because that's how they've always been done. Organizations lose so much by failing to allow room or time for creative solutions.

❖ Finally, followers need to make a commitment to **excellence**. Robert Kennedy kept the following quote on his desk: "Some see things as they are and say why. I see things as they could be and say why not?"

When GRACE - guidance, respect, accountability, creativity and excellence - is directed towards the development of creative followers:

1. Creative followers blossom in unexpected and rewarding ways.

2. The program benefits because it gains the best effort of all involved.

3. It makes better leaders. Thus we have a new definition for leadership: the ability to develop, encourage and inspire creative followers.

These resources reflect a paradigm shift in leadership, moving from a management focus of controlling and directing to a visionary leadership concept of empowering and enabling others to create the future.

As visionary leaders, we must mobilize and enable people to succeed in more creative ways. We can be pivotal in encouraging shared leadership as well as in the development of the group as a team. Most critical will be our ability as leaders to truly value and celebrate the successes of others. Today's world demands that we be proactive in dealing successfully with the significant changes occurring in society.

Our role as leaders, in the final analysis, is to be instrumental in developing other's potential to move us towards our mission and goals. When we become the catalyst motivating capable and creative people to community action, when we put in place the systems that will allow them to be successful, when we advocate for their involvement in meaningful activities that are mission-driven and when we celebrate their successes as we would our own - then we will have chosen the path that leads to an infinitely stronger and vitalized community.

You as a community leader can make a difference in your organization, your community and your country. Enhancing those leadership skills is what the rest of this book is all about.

REFERENCES

1. Kouzes and Posner, *The Leadership Challenge,* Jossey-Bass Publishers, 1990
2. Covey, Stephen, *The Seven Habits of Highly Effective People,* Simon and Schuster, 1989
3. W. Chan Kim and Renée Mauborgne, *Harvard Business Review,* July-August, 1992.
4. Marilyn MacKenzie, "Creative Followership" published in the Spring 1989 edition of *Voluntary Action Leadership*

CHAPTER SEVEN
THE GROUP LEADER

TASK RESPONSIBILITIES

When someone agrees to take on the role of leader or chair, people often assume that the person requires no orientation since they have prior involvement with the group. Quite the contrary - a new chair requires orientation because the nature of the position changes significantly.

What then are the major functions of a chair?

* task responsibilities
* group development responsibilities
* nurturing individual members

GETTING THE JOB DONE

This is what the committee or group is created for! To accomplish this responsibility, the chairperson:

* calls meetings
* sees that progress is recorded and reported as needed
* shapes the agenda and selects activities that will help
* the committee to develop as a team and achieve its goals
* plans the work of the group and evaluates progress
* delegates work to be done between meetings
* guides discussion at the meetings

Some of these tasks, like planning or agenda creation, are shared with group members. The skilled chairperson is guided by the belief that joint effort produces better results than the efforts of a single leader. This approach takes more time and attention, but pays off significantly in terms of members' commitment to the tasks that accomplish committee goals.

For the past six months, Clayton has chaired the newly created Support Services Committee of a local health charity. He agreed to take the leadership role because he believes passionately in the cause and was excited that he could really make a difference in the lives of people locally. The first few meetings were OK, although Clayton felt that people could have been more enthusiastic about the ambitious plans that he outlined. In fact, Clayton was so excited about his idea for a community meeting that he went ahead and organized it after the second meeting.

Now things are not going well at all. Attendance at committee meetings has dropped and people show little enthusiasm about participating. In fact, he had to cancel the last meeting because most people couldn't come. Clayton feels resentful that he is putting in so much time and effort and no one else on the committee is helping. What to do?

THE ISSUE FOR CLAYTON IS TWO-FOLD.

He tried to move the new group forward in a direction that reflected his dream and his vision for the committee rather than discovering what the other members might wish to see as goals for support services.

In his enthusiasm to get on with the task, he also neglected to delegate to the others. By carrying the load himself, he failed to gain their involvement and thereby their support.

It's mighty hard to generate enthusiasm for a journey if you don't have any idea where you're planning to go.

Vision without action is merely a dream,
Action without vision just passes the time,
Vision with action can change the world.
Joel Arthur Baker

From an organizational perspective a board must articulate and affirm the mission and mandate as the foundation for all activity of the organization. In the case of committees that are mandated by a board, the overall purpose and terms of reference may be dictated, but the committee itself must wrestle with developing a common vision for its journey together.

A new group leader or committee chair may fall into the trap of assuming responsibility for tasks that should be done by group members themselves. By carrying this load, the chair is doing no one any favours - the members, the chair or the organization itself.

The one-person committee or the leader who neglects to delegate to the group prevents effective member participation. This type of one-person show frequently results in leadership frustration and burnout. It is crucial to delegate and to involve others, for by sharing the load, members feel a sense of ownership and pleasure in both the completion of the task and the personal commitment to the cause.

Volunteer organizations are particularly dependent on well-functioning committees and task forces. By delegating most of the work to appropriate committees, organizations not only share the workload but involve people who bring new ideas, different skills and interests. Involvement at the committee level enhances new members' learning about the organization and provides opportunities for increased satisfaction.

The tendency today is to reduce the number of standing (ongoing) committees and to strike task forces to deal with specific issues or projects as required. This is responsive to the fact that people today are reluctant to make a long-term commitment. By contributing their expertise on a short-term task force, they feel a sense of accomplishment and may be open to an additional involvement at another time.

A Word about Delegation

Effective delegation isn't easy. There is probably more grief and more time wasted because of poor delegation than any other activity undertaken by people in leadership positions. A chairperson or president is ultimately responsible for the work of the group, committee or board and so wants to be sure all work is well done. At the same time, it is foolish to attempt to do all the work independently. By involving others, the load is lessened. It is important to remember that commitment is built in others through their involvement. People who offer to help, however, need guidance. For an individual, group or committee to act successfully the following are needed:

Select tasks for people that are appropriate to the skills, knowledge and experience they bring. People want to feel good about their contribution.

Explain the results you seek and the deadlines to get the work done. Be specific - "Please prepare three recommendations for me by Friday." There is nothing more discouraging than to have work rejected at its completion. Time spent initially clarifying and confirming what is wanted is time well spent.

Be prepared to spend time at the beginning of a project, to clarify the task and instruct members of the group. This prevents mistakes and misunderstandings that are difficult to correct.

Encourage people to use their own "grey cells" to decide how to solve the problem or organize the work. Give people freedom to think and be creative.

Explain the purpose of the assignment and how it fits into the big picture of the project. People are motivated when they understand the reasons for their effort.

The Big Picture:

Two men were working on a construction site. Each was doing essentially the same job, but one seemed distracted while the other attacked his work with enthusiasm and obvious pride. When asked what they were doing, the first said he was only a stone cutter - the second said he was building a cathedral that would stand for a thousand years.

Be sure to follow up on mutually determined deadlines. Set up checkpoints for big projects.

Trust people to complete work as assigned. If problems develop, don't rush in to rescue the person but rather encourage him to resolve the problem by suggesting alternate solutions and recommendations.

Help people to learn from their mistakes by reviewing the situation and asking them how they would handle it differently next time. "What have we learned from this mistake that we can use next time?"

Praise work well done.

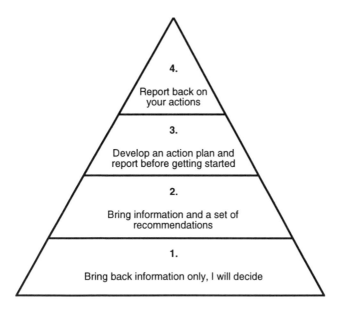

Your major concern is that work is well done. At the same time, as a "people developer", you want to be sure that as confidence and experience increase, you provide more opportunities to act with less direction from you. The Limits of Action pyramid provides guidelines.

1. With a new committee member you will need to offer lots of advice and direction. Ask that person to bring back information to you so that you can decide or resolve an issue. It is important to involve the new person in the process of decision making by thinking out loud and enabling her to appreciate what goes into making your choice.

2. With a slightly more experienced individual, you might expect not only the needed information but a set of recommendations concerning the issue. You would review the recommendations with the individual, making suggestions or asking questions to stimulate thought and understanding.

3. In the case of a well experienced member you want to support considerable freedom to act and an acknowledgement of your respect for her independence. You would encourage the individual not only to make recommendations, but to develop an action plan derived from those recommendations. You would review the plan with the individual, again posing questions that raise alternatives.

4. Finally, with your most trusted people, you encourage them to act independently and report outcomes or results to you. This implies an enormous amount of confidence based on their skill and experience.

The limits of action for committees are often set out in the terms of reference for that committee but application of the same principles should be part of every interaction with volunteers. Because people's commitment grows with their involvement, you will want to increase opportunities for meaningful engagement.

PLANNING FOR SUCCESSFUL MEETINGS

Too often people attend meetings, only to leave at the end feeling they were a waste of time and energy. Why is this such a frequent lament? Common meeting complains include:

"We never start on time"
"Meetings drag on and don't accomplish anything"
"Only a few people have something concrete to do"
"We keep rehashing old business"
"Some people dominate discussions"
"People come unprepared or fail to follow through on work"

The list goes on and on. But take heart - meetings can be both productive and fun. When there is a compelling reason to meet regularly, the benefits to the group are legion. Meetings can:

- provide members with up-to-date information
- develop sense of team and group development
- encourage broader participation in decision making
- spread the workload
- stimulate more creative solutions
- enhance and improves initial ideas
- encourage leadership growth of members
- develop commitment to group decisions

Be very sure there is actually a reason to meet. If a telephone call, memo, fax, letter or brief conversation can provide the necessary information or recommendations for action - then by all means go with that alternative. Meeting "just because we always have" is the worst possible reason for holding meetings. You might want to use the following guide to help you decide if you really need to meet, and if so, plan the structure of the meeting.

Guideline for Planning a Meeting

1. Purpose: Why are we meeting? What outcomes or key results do we hope to achieve?

2. Is a meeting necessary to accomplish our purpose and desired results? □ Yes □ No

   What methods other than a meeting might accomplish our purpose?

3. Participants: Who should attend?

4. Agenda: Have I arranged for input from members? How can I group the agenda items to maximize discussion? What time will be required?

5. Physical Set-up: What is the best seating arrangement for this meeting? What equipment do we need?

6. Key Meeting Roles: Who will I assign to be:

   Meeting Facilitator   Recorder
   Timekeeper   Scribe (if required)

7. Evaluation: How will we evaluate the process and the results of the meeting?

The forms in this section provide the framework for a meeting management system that is efficient and effective. The system is designed to:

* encourage the involvement of all members
* ensure that members come to meetings with the information they need to make good decisions
* reduce the time spent on verbal reporting
* simplify the recording of minutes
* focus on decisions and next steps
* reduce the workload in writing, distributing minutes

If typed minutes are not absolutely necessary (and often they are not), this system is wonderfully efficient. When written in black ink, they photocopy clearly, saving considerable secretarial and administrative time. The system will be of particular interest to leaders who have limited secretarial support for meetings. The components include:

Group Agenda Planner
Meeting Agenda
Meeting Attendance Record
Meeting Decision and Action Record
Report for Decision Making

GROUP AGENDA PLANNER (FORM 1)

The purpose of this document is to give all members an opportunity to help shape the agenda for upcoming meetings. It asks people to indicate issues for discussion and the time needed for each. Just before the end of the meeting the Recorder fills in the identified agenda items for the next meeting, photocopies and circulates the document to committee members for any additional suggestions. When they are returned (at least two weeks before the next meeting), the chair will then develop the final agenda.

MEETING AGENDA (FORM 2)

The agenda is completed (in black ink for photocopying), with not only the subject topic, but also a brief description outlining the item and the desired outcomes. If we treated menus like we often do agendas, a menu would simply read "meat". One person might assume it's chicken while another expected lobster! Without a specific topic focus, members may interpret differently the nature of the proposed discussion. A member who is bringing a recommendation to the committee for a decision or who wishes to report on progress should complete and attach a Report for Decision Making (Form 5) to be mailed along with the agenda.

MEETING ATTENDANCE RECORD (FORM 3)

At the beginning of the meeting the Recorder completes the top portion of the Meeting Attendance Record and fills in the names of those members who sent regrets. The form and a black ink pen are passed around for people to "sign in" with their names, telephone and fax numbers. If members represent community groups they might include the name of the organization. At the end the Recorder fills in the date and location of the next meeting and indicates who will be contacting absent people. Attached to top of the minutes, this tool enables people to connect easily following the meeting.

MEETING DECISION AND ACTION RECORD (FORM 4)

What really needs to be recorded in the minutes? As a general practice, minutes often include unnecessary details of meeting discussion, creating numerous opportunities for people to later disagree or misinterpret details. Too often we spend valuable time rehashing the decisions of previous meetings rather than dealing with agenda items of current and future significance.

What is the real purpose of minutes? There are two key reasons for taking minutes - to record the decisions made by the group and to record the resulting action steps required, including by whom and by when.

The Meeting Decision and Action Record form is designed to enable the Recorder to legibly highlight key points and decisions. Items are numbered to correspond to the agenda. Any written reports or supporting documents become addenda to the minutes. The formal agenda should be completed a few minutes before the meeting is scheduled to end so that the minutes can be photocopied and distributed. People highlight the actions to which they have committed and (if they wish) approve the minutes as recorded before they leave. This certainly prevents dickering about decisions and discussions at the next meeting. No more mountains of paper to be typed, complaints about not receiving minutes, and excuses that "I thought John was supposed to do that". Should typed minutes be a requirement for the formal record, then one can use the same format and have them typed following the meeting.

REPORT FOR DECISION MAKING (FORM 5)

Establish a group norm that all individual or committee reports and recommendations to the group must be submitted in a written summary. The Report for Decision Making is completed by the appropriate member(s) and included with the meeting agenda that is mailed to the group. This allows people to be prepared for the meeting. It also requests that anyone with concerns or questions speak with the person who is making the recommendations prior to the meeting. Clarifying minor concerns before the meeting speeds up the reporting process and allows more time for discussion and decision making.

GROUP AGENDA PLANNER

Committee/Group: **Date:**

Items to bring forward from our meeting: **Time Required:**

Topic:_____

Desired Outcomes:_____

                          ☐ Info only   ☐ Decision

Topic:_____

Desired Outcomes:_____

                          ☐ Info only   ☐ Decision

Topic:_____

Desired Outcomes:_____

                          ☐ Info only   ☐ Decision

Please list in order of priority topics (with desired outcomes) you want included on our

meeting agenda for: _____

Item: **Time Required:**

1. Topic:_____

Desired Outcomes:_____

                          ☐ Info only   ☐ Decision

2. Topic:_____

Desired Outcomes:_____

                          ☐ Info only   ☐ Decision

Name: _____ Tel: _____ Fax:_____

Please include any completed Report for Decision Making forms that you want mailed with the final agenda.

FORM 1

GROUP AGENDA PLANNER

Committee/Group: **Bazaar Committee**   Date: **Oct. 17/93**

Items to bring forward from our meeting: Time Required:

Topic: **1994 Bazaar**   **15 min**

Desired Outcomes: **• determine new location • find convenor**

☑ Info only ☐ Decision

Topic: **Evaluation of meeting**   **15 min**

Desired Outcomes: **• member assumes resp. fn planning**

☑ Info only ☐ Decision

Topic: **Recognition Dinner**   **10 min.**

Desired Outcomes: **• Select chair • determine date**

☐ Info only ☒ Decision

Please list in order of priority topics (with desired outcomes) you want included on our meeting agenda for: **Nov. 28/93**

Item: Time Required:

1. Topic: **Schedule of Meetings**   **5 min.**

Desired Outcomes: **Set dates for year**

☐ Info only ☒ Decision

2. Topic: **Board development training**

Desired Outcomes: **• training session commitment for late fall.**

☐ Info only ☐ Decision

Name: **Danny P.**   Tel: **225-7067** Fax: **225-7000**

Please include any completed Report for Decision Making forms that you want mailed with the final agenda.

FORM 1

MEETING AGENDA

Committee/Group: _____

Meeting Date: _____Location: _____

Start Time: _____Adjourn Time: _____

Chair:_____Recorder:_____

Timekeeper:_____Scribe:_____

Topic/Item   Person Speaking re Issue & Time

_____

Desired Outcomes:_____

_____Report Attached: □

_____

Desired Outcomes:_____

_____Report Attached: □

_____

Desired Outcomes:_____

_____Report Attached: □

_____

Desired Outcomes:_____

_____Report Attached: □

_____

Desired Outcomes:_____

_____Report Attached: □

_____

Desired Outcomes:_____

_____Report Attached: □

_____

Desired Outcomes:_____

Please contact the appropriate person prior to the meeting if you have questions about the attached reports.

FORM 2

MEETING AGENDA

Committee/Group: _Creaky Knees Bazaar Committee_
Meeting Date: _Oct 17/93_   Location: _C.K. Centre_
Start Time: _2 pm_   Adjourn Time: _4 pm_
Chair: _Sally Single_   Recorder: _Maud_
Timekeeper: _Willard_   Scribe: _(we'll see)_

Topic/Item   Person Speaking re Issue & Time

 # 1 _Warm-up (Surprise!)_
Desired Outcomes: _get to know each other better,_
introduce 2 new members   Report Attached: ☐

 # 2 _Information Items - reports_
Desired Outcomes: _• common understanding of_
expense policies; upcoming dates   Report Attached: ☒

 # 3 _Membership Policy for Bazaar Committee_
Desired Outcomes: _• clarification of eligibility (Maud)_
• decision to expand/maintain   Report Attached: ☒

 # 4 _1994 Bazaar_
Desired Outcomes: _• determine theme,_
• set dates • choose leader   Report Attached: ☐

 # 5 _How are we doing? Evaluation_
Desired Outcomes: _• see how we can work_
together • pat ourselves on   Report Attached: ☐
back

_____
Desired Outcomes:_____
_____Report Attached: ☐

_____
Desired Outcomes:_____

Please contact the appropriate person prior to the meeting if you have questions about the attached reports.

FORM 2

MEETING ATTENDANCE RECORD

Committee/Group:_____

Date:_____

Names of those Present: Telephone/Fax

_____

_____

_____

_____

_____

_____

_____

_____

_____

_____

_____

Chaired by: _____

Regrets: To Be Called By:

_____

_____

_____

_____

_____

Next Meeting: _____

Location: _____

Guests to be invited: By Whom:

_____

_____

FORM 3

MEETING ATTENDANCE RECORD

Committee/Group: _Creaky Knees Bazaar Committee_

Date: _Oct 17/93_

Names of those Present: Telephone/Fax

Carla Cotton	276-9201
Willard Wooly	246-0777
Maud Schwepps	372-0764
Nellie Needle	886-9583
Paul Patchwork	276-9000
Jim Brown	fax 339-2071

Chaired by: _Sandra Single_   _225-1892_

Regrets: To Be Called By:

Fred Fuzzlebutt   Paul

Joan James   Willard

Next Meeting: _November 28/93_   _2 pm._

Location: _Creaky Knees Retirement Centre_

Guests to be invited: By Whom:

Mayor's Wife   _Sandra S._

FORM 3

MEETING DECISION AND ACTION RECORD

Meeting Minutes for:_____

Agenda Item #	Decision/Motion	Next Steps	By When	By Whom

FORM 4

MEETING DECISION AND ACTION RECORD

Meeting Minutes for: _Creaky Knees Bazaar Committee_

Agenda Item #	Decision/Motion	Next Steps	By When	By Whom
1.	We need new warm up ideas	① research ideas	Dec	Will
2.	Policies are fine. Need to be circulated. Will develop a manual	① Check other centre	Jan	Sal
3.	Membership policy approved. Report 93-3 attached	• Include in manual	Jan	Nellie
4.	1994 Theme discussion "Bazaaring Towards a New Century"			
5.	Decided to defer discussion to next meeting	Carla to research ideas	NM	Carla

REPORT FOR DECISION MAKING

From:_____ Date: _____ Report No._____

For Information: ☐   Recommendation for Decision: ☐

Topic: _____

_____

_____

Background: _____

_____

_____

_____

_____

_____

Considerations/Pros & Cons: _____

_____

_____

_____

_____

_____

Action Already Taken/To Take: _____

_____

_____

_____

Recommendations/Desired Outcomes: _____

_____

_____

_____

Concerns/questions prior to meeting call: _____

at _____ before _____

FORM 5

REPORT FOR DECISION MAKING

Task Force

From: Maudie Schwepps   Date: Oct 2/93   Report No. 93-3

For Information: ☐   Recommendation for Decision: ☒

Topic: Need for new policy outlining eligibility for membership on Creaky Knees Bazaar Committee.

Background: Historically only paid-up members of the Creaky Knees Centre were eligible to work on the committee. In recent years, other people have offered to help

Considerations/Pros & Cons: PRO: is major fundraiser, needs lots of help & new blood. new people may result in more people becoming members, a time for new ideas.
CON: Old Timers may feel that non-members don't belong or are using their resources

Action Already Taken/To Take: 3 current members have "interviewed" a sample of members to ask their views. 83% were delighted to encourage new people to help.

Recommendations/Desired Outcomes: That membership on CK Bazaar Committee + participation at the sale be opened to include any interested people.

Concerns/questions prior to meeting call: Maudie
at 886-8585 before October 12, 1993

FORM 5

Assigning Roles

The first section of this book contained information about the task and relationship roles that members play in a group. Facilitation is enhanced when the following meeting roles are specifically defined.

Chair as Facilitator: The leader or chair of the group is most commonly the person who facilitates the meeting, focusing on the dynamics of the process. Should the leader wish to comment on the content of the discussion, it is important to indicate this change of "hats" to participants.

Members as Facilitators: All participants have a personal responsibility for practising appropriate behaviours as well as a collective responsibility to help other participants stay on track in a positive way.

Timekeeper: One member is assigned to monitor the length of discussion and alert the group to the remaining time for agenda items.

Scribe: The facilitator may at times during the meeting choose to have a scribe to record group discussion on flipchart paper. This is especially helpful when the group is in the creative mode of brainstorming, doing a force field analysis or discussing the pros and cons of an issue. Comments should be posted for reference during the meeting. These sheets may be transcribed at the conclusion of the meeting and retained as background material for further discussion or action. The scribe does not participate in or in any way control the discussion, but simply records verbatim people's contributions.

Recorder: The person taking minutes documents the key decisions made and action steps required for each agenda item, highlighting who is responsible and by what date.

Checklist of Meeting Leader Tasks

Prior to the Meeting: do I?
- ☐ Request input for the agenda from committee members
- ☐ Develop clear purpose and objectives for the meeting
- ☐ Identify key results or desired outcomes
- ☐ Mail agenda, background material and minutes well in advance
- ☐ Follow-up with members to ensure assigned tasks are done
- ☐ Check that physical space is appropriate, with required equipment
- ☐ Arrange for necessary materials and information to be available
- ☐ Ensure that key people are there to provide information and make decisions

When Starting the Meeting, do I?
- ☐ Start on time. Waiting for late arrivals is unfair to those present
- ☐ Begin with a warm-up activity
- ☐ Outline purpose or reasons for the meeting
- ☐ Distribute agenda and minutes (if not mailed prior)
- ☐ Discuss and affirm specific objectives and desired outcomes
- ☐ State time lines and agree on any rules of procedure

When Facilitating the Meeting, do I?
- ☐ Follow the agenda
- ☐ Assess priorities if necessary
- ☐ Actively listen, paraphrase and restate opinions and ideas expressed
- ☐ Encourage other members to actively listen
- ☐ Act as a traffic cop. Keep the discussion on topic
  - refer back to the objectives if people go off topic
  - keep note of who has spoken and who wants to speak
  - allow one person at a time to speak
  - remind group re: time constraints
- ☐ Give credit where it's due by acknowledging people's ideas
- ☐ Encourage participation and contributions from all
- ☐ Summarize accomplishments as decisions are reached, preferably on flipchart paper

Towards the End of the Meeting, do I?
- ☐ Summarize accomplishments and thank people for their contribution
- ☐ Check results with desired outcomes
- ☐ Remind members of follow-up required
- ☐ Encourage members to identify agenda items for next meeting
- ☐ Set date for next meeting (unless already scheduled)
- ☐ Evaluate meeting and group process.

Tasks of a Facilitator

- Create and maintain a warm and trusting climate

- Focus group activity on definition and accomplishment of goals and objectives

- Help keep the process on track

- Present and receive information, feelings and observations in a variety of ways:

  - questions
  - exercises and activities
  - formats

- Explore a variety of options for problem solving and decision making

- Encourage balanced participation by all group members

- Build individual support for full group decisions

- Model responsible risk-taking by

  - sharing leadership
  - asking for feedback
  - acknowledging resistance

Planning the Meeting Structure

Building the Agenda

The structure of any meeting falls into three parts: the opening phase, the key discussion and decision making phase and the closing phase. Carefully planning these phases by means of an effective agenda and a thoughtful process will maximize people's participation and result in increased productivity and satisfaction. The model on the next page illustrates the key components of these three phases.

Pre-Meeting

Additional pre-meeting tasks are outlined in the Leader Checklist. The agenda is the master plan that sets the stage for a productive meeting. People will only participate regularly if they feel good, generate energy and have opportunity to use their creativity. Sadly enough, these are the very qualities that are so often missing in meetings! Carefully structuring the agenda enables the chair to accomplish these results.

By encouraging members to suggest agenda topics you will build ownership of the issues. It is important to identify the key results or desired outcomes for each agenda item that requires a decision by the group.

Reports that require a decision should be pre-circulated with the agenda so that participants have an opportunity to reflect on the issues.

Structure of a Meeting

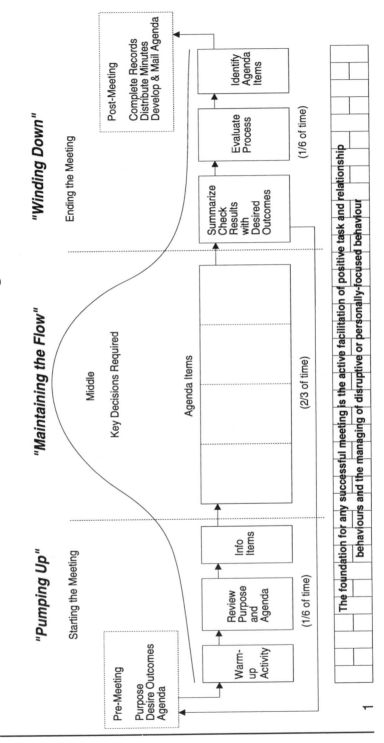

"Pumping Up"

Starting the Meeting

Pre-Meeting

Purpose
Desire Outcomes
Agenda

"Maintaining the Flow"

Middle

Key Decisions Required

"Winding Down"

Ending the Meeting

Post-Meeting

Complete Records
Distribute Minutes
Develop & Mail Agenda

Warm-up Activity

Review Purpose and Agenda

Info Items

Agenda Items

Summarize Check Results with Desired Outcomes

Evaluate Process

Identify Agenda Items

(1/6 of time)

(2/3 of time)

(1/6 time)

The foundation for any successful meeting is the active facilitation of positive task and relationship behaviours and the managing of disruptive or personally-focused behaviour

1

Meetings involve three types of tasks - informing, deciding and discussing. An effective agenda will "batch" these types of items together. The traditional agenda format of dealing with "Business Arising" first often results in a premature discussion of issues that are included in later agenda items. Eliminate the headings "Old Business/Business Arising" and build these items into the agenda topics themselves. The open-ended practice of requesting "New Business" is a hangover from the days when a chair failed to involve the group in developing the agenda. The closing part of the meeting allows members to suggest new business for discussion at the next meeting.

Sequencing Agenda Items

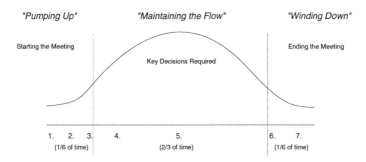

PUMPING UP

1. Warm up
2. Minutes (if necessary)
   Purpose and Desired Outcomes
3. Information Items: Batched together for brief reporting

The importance of an informal warm up activity can't be overemphasized. Spending ten minutes at the beginning of a session creates a relaxed and welcoming atmosphere, helps people know each other better and is a transition from earlier activities to the tasks at hand. It is important that the warm up be accepted as a legitimate part of the agenda, not an excuse for arriving late. Suggestions for warm up activities are described later in this chapter.

Moving through the Middle

The bulk of the meeting should focus on developing creative solutions to important issues. Sequence topics for discussion so that items follow a logical information flow.

4. Order topics from the easiest to the more difficult, dealing with easy decisions upfront to set a good pace and build a momentum of early successes.

5. Try to deal with only one very contentious issue, scheduling it no later than midway through the decision period so that there is ample time to debate the alternatives and build consensus.

Winding Down

The final portion of the meeting is an opportunity to "rebind" the group, especially if the previous decisions polarized participants. Celebrate progress by briefly summarizing outcomes, checking against desired results. Build commitment to improving group participation by evaluating the process of the meeting.

6. A simple technique is to write "What went well?" and "What might we do differently?" as headings on flipchart paper. The group agrees to continue practising one positive item and selects two for attention at the next session. This evaluation and the commitments to improve should be recorded in the minutes.

7. Spend a few moments building the next meeting agenda together. Encourage people to propose new topics for inclusion at the next meeting. They may want to use the Group Agenda Planner that is part of the recordkeeping system. This reaps enormous dividends in terms of member commitment to the process.

Finishing on a light-hearted note means that people will leave in a positive frame of mind. Suggestions for creatively recognizing their participation are in the next chapter.

By planning for meetings in the cyclical pattern outlined the Meeting Model, a chair generates a future-oriented approach to working with groups. Once the agenda has been finalized, it is mailed to members along with any reports.

REFERENCES

1. Adapted from Kayser, Thomas, *Mining Group Gold,* Pfeiffer and Company, 1990.

CHAPTER EIGHT
GROUP DEVELOPMENT

LEADER RESPONSIBILITIES

> *Coming Together is a Beginning*
> *Keeping Together is Progress*
> *Working Together is Success*
> *Source unknown*

When people first meet, they are a collection of individuals. It is only as they work together and get to know one another that they become a group. The chairperson assists the group by keeping it to set rules and norms for participation, problem-solving and conflict resolution. The chairperson guides the group as it forms, recognizing that rebellion and controversy are healthy and desirable in a group.

STAGES OF GROUP DEVELOPMENT

Regardless of how able and sophisticated individual members may be, groups need time to evolve into a cohesive unit. Just as the caterpillar must spin a cocoon before emerging as a spectacular butterfly, so must groups work their way through the stages of development.

There are numerous theories describing how groups form and develop. Although various theorists may use different terms to explain the stages, the actual phases are typically the same. While Tuckman[1] described these stages as Forming, Storming, Norming, Performing and Adjourning, we have equated the stages with our own life cycle. The stages are sequential and developmental. All groups progress through these phases, although some may, in fact, get stuck in one or another!

Stage One: Infancy/Childhood (Forming)

Jack has been a member of the Lions Club for several years. He recently agreed to organize a group of members to form a Special Projects Committee. Their task is to research and recommend new service projects. Jack was careful to invite several new members to join the group.

The committee has met twice and Jack is quite discouraged. Few people, mostly the old hands, say anything at all, and even then, it seems during the meetings that the ball is always bouncing back to him as leader for a decision. People are certainly polite to each other, but their participation seems superficial.

What is really happening?

When people first come together as a group, they usually don't know much about what they and the group will be doing. In this beginning stage of group development they are preoccupied with attempting to learn about their interpersonal relationships in the group and to orient themselves to the task.

The behaviours that are typical and which you will observe in this stage include:

- people stick with people they know
- people often arrive at the last moment
- people tend to be very polite
- people direct comments to the facilitator, not other members
- little conflict or energetic discussion
- people tend to either talk a lot, or very little
- most decisions are made by the group leader or a very few members

What you see does not always reflect what's happening under-neath. In the beginning, people are unclear about what they will be doing and what is expected of them. Even though they may have met each other before, they make many assumptions about other members' behaviour and attitudes. Because people defer to the leader to make decisions, there is little or no commitment to decisions made by the group.

Privately, people are wondering:

- why was I asked to be here?
- what will I be doing?
- will I know how to do the job?
- do the others really want me?
- what if I say the wrong thing?

WHAT IS REQUIRED TO HELP THE GROUP ALONG?

❖ people need to know **why** they are there

> Orient people to terms of reference for the committee and why they were invited

❖ people need to know what is **expected** of them

- the agenda and how discussion will be handled
- purpose and tasks for each meeting
- norms for this group
- individual member's expectations

❖ people need to **learn about each other**, what they can expect of other members and whether they can trust them with their honest feelings. This can be achieved by using:

- warm ups
- Window of Work described later in this chapter
- active listening

❖ people need to **express their ideas and feelings.** This will be encouraged by:

- ◆ a meeting format that includes lots of interaction in pairs, triads or small groups
- ◆ building on the comments of others, acknowledging their contributions

Stage Two: Adolescence (Storming)

For the past year Susan has been on the Art Council's program committee. When the chair recently resigned, she reluctantly agreed to assume the leadership role. Susan is appalled by the very childish behaviour of many of the members. Last night was the absolute end when two members argued at length about which speaker had been invited for the Founders Day Festival. When they checked the minutes to resolve the issue, the "loser" was real disgruntled. Susan feels that somehow they all blame her for what happened. Unless she can find someone to offer suggestions, she is ready to throw in the towel!

This stage is like adolescence. On a process level, people now need to discover how they measure up to others in the group, how important they are to the group and the group to them. The most common way for people to do this is for members to try to influence others, or react to other's influencing. People are trying to gain acceptance for their ideas, and in doing this deal with their own and others' needs for control.

The content issues the group is dealing with are focused on organizing the tasks to be done. People are required to modify their ideas and opinions to suit the larger group. This is usually characterized by people needing to be very clear about the structural content of the task at hand. Because people are uncomfortable with the conflict that often happens in this stage, some people may not participate at all in discussion, while a few try to dominate.

❖ people focus on their own comments, and don't usually clarify what other people mean

❖ people understand decisions differently or they may not even remember

❖ differences in opinion about past events often need to be resolved by looking at the minutes

❖ behaviour patterns have emerged:
   ◆ where people sit
   ◆ who supports which people
   ◆ who is reticent about participating
   ◆ who challenges, is in conflict

❖ people do not accept personal responsibility for what happens and they blame others, especially the leader

❖ people's true feelings are not expressed at the meeting, but afterwards, in the parking lot or in telephone calls

WHAT IS REALLY HAPPENING UNDER THE SURFACE? PEOPLE ARE DEALING WITH UNDERLYING ISSUES. THESE MAY BE:

❖ feeling that they are not valued

❖ feeling insecure and without influence

❖ concerned with their own needs for acceptance, protection from criticism and recognition

❖ struggling with: "Why am I here?", "Who's in charge?", "How can I influence?"

❖ easily influenced by those they support

❖ unaware that this stage is normal in group development. They blame others for problems.

According to Tuckman, this stage always happens in the group's development. On the other hand, there is some controversy that Stage Two may not necessarily occur if norms are developed, shared leadership occurs and if plans for increasing resolution are clear. When members are comfortable with each other, are able to express their feelings about both the content and process and have some understanding of group development, then this stage will be relatively short.

When there is a real power struggle among group members, Stage Two can be very angry and prolonged. The leader and other members of the group should enhance this by:

- ensuring that Stage One issues have been addressed
- asking people for their opinions and ideas
- paraphrasing and summarizing ideas, demonstrating that people have been heard
- recording suggestions to acknowledge contributions
- listening intently to people's concerns and working with the full group to solve them

The group feedback form, in Chapter Four How Are We Doing would be a useful tool to get people really talking.

STAGE THREE: EARLY ADULTHOOD (NORMING)

When the group moves out of the Adolescent Stage people demonstrate greater cohesion in their interpersonal relationships. They become more comfortable articulating how they feel about working together and openly sharing and discussing their varied communication styles. On a process level, the focus for people at this stage is concentrated on how the group is operating.

The emphasis on the content level relates to the data flow between members, soliciting and giving feedback and exploring ideas related to the task. If this stage is achieved by a group, creativity is high and people openly share information about both task and process. People feel good about working together effectively as a group. As a result they may resist change because they want things to stay the same.

- ◆ people ask questions of each other
- ◆ people are willing to listen and to change their opinions
- ◆ people may share how they are feeling about the group
- ◆ this may be followed by some discomfort and silence
- ◆ others may respond "don't feel that way..."
- ◆ others will share "when you do this...I feel..."
- ◆ others may propose "it would help me if we ..."
- ◆ people may suggest "Let's try to..."
- ◆ changes are suggested to help people listen, share, etc.

WHAT IS HAPPENING UNDER THE SURFACE?

- ❖ talking about feelings is a new phase for the group and sometimes people are unsure how to respond

- ❖ people may be defensive about other's reactions, feeling that they are being criticized

- ❖ people identify with other's feelings

- ❖ people feel a sense of relief that they can talk about their own and other's feelings

- ❖ as the group becomes more accepting of differences, people's confidence grows

- ❖ people have come to care about each other

- ❖ with increased understanding and acceptance, people are open to changing their own behaviour

Openly accepting what people feel is vital at this stage. In the beginning people may have difficulty clearly expressing how they are feeling. They need to be encouraged to be responsive and accepting, responding to the feeling, not the accusation or blame. It is important when someone discloses dissatisfaction that this be accepted, because if their honest effort to express feelings is not supported, they will not be willing to be open and things will continue to be swept under the rug.

Towards the end of this stage it is typical that agreements about how the group will work together become the group norms, the accepted way in which the group works together.

STAGE FOUR: GLORIOUS ADULTHOOD (PERFORMING)

Tuckman believes that the Performing Stage is not always reached by groups. During this stage the group not only works effectively on its goals, tasks and objectives, but also respects the needs of its members by being sensitive to the process. This stage is characterized by members' interdependence on a process level. They are able to work together in a variety of ways, moving in and out of the leadership role. Shared leadership is the norm. On a task level they are very productive, demonstrating creative problem solving.

THE TYPICAL BEHAVIOURS THAT YOU WILL OBSERVE INCLUDE:

- different people play a lead role at different times
- ability to influence is shared, based most often on ideas
- people are comfortable about asking for clarification
- people rephrase others' comments
- people acknowledge contributions
- less tension, lots of laughter
- openness to comment about task, process and feelings

❖ people feel a high level of comfort and trust with each other

❖ competition has diminished and people feel good about acknowledging each other's contributions

❖ people want to develop solutions that are good for everyone in the group

❖ people are comfortable raising issues that might impede the task in process

❖ the group feels proud of how it works together

KNOWING THIS, WHAT IS REQUIRED AT THIS POINT?

The sad part is that this stage does not last forever! Groups often move on to the next stage or revert back to previous stages if new members or goals are introduced.

STAGE FIVE: DEATH (ADJOURNING)

Doug has chaired his health charity branch for nine years and wants desperately to pass the reins to someone else. Unfortunately, no one else on the board will agree to be chair. They tried recruiting new people a few times over the years but no one stayed long, so it really wasn't worth the effort. It has been particularly discouraging as chair this past year because attendance at the meetings is sporadic, people are often late and even when they do come, they aren't willing to really do anything. Last night's meeting was the final straw. Two people showed up and one of them had to leave after coffee. What's a chair to do?

Yes, groups do die. They don't necessarily last forever, nor should they! The important thing to recognize is that there is a time to come and a time to go. This stage finds people terminating task functions and separating themselves from relationships.

THE TYPICAL BEHAVIOURS YOU WILL OBSERVE ARE:

- ◆ people are inattentive
- ◆ little commitment to discussion
- ◆ no new suggestions or solutions
- ◆ problems are repeatedly approached in the same way
- ◆ people start side conversations
- ◆ people keep looking at watches
- ◆ people "prepare" to leave before it's over

WHAT IS REQUIRED AT THIS POINT?

This stage is very uncomfortable for people. It is important that there be a sense of closure, of pulling all the loose ends together and acknowledging that "the time has come". It would be important to have an evaluation of the process and the group as well as a celebration of accomplishments.

From a leader's perspective, it is suggested that Tuckman's model of group development is most effective as a learning tool when the group is in Stage Three. Before that, it may be of little interest or create additional conflicts, after that it is unnecessary.

MOTIVATING MEMBERS AND CREATING A TEAM

Perhaps you have recently agreed to chair a committee or group. Much has been written about leadership, the style and qualities that make effective leaders and how they interact with others. As a chairperson you will need to focus on motivating others to work as a team.

1. CLARIFY THE GROUP EXPECTATIONS:

Know the terms of reference and mandate assigned to your group or committee. A written statement of the purpose and desired outcomes of the work of your group will prevent any confusion about the task you were assigned or the framework within which you work. Don't agree to take on a task as chair unless you and they are very clear about the work to be done.

2. RECRUIT THE RIGHT PEOPLE; REACH OUT TO OTHERS WHO MIGHT HELP:

Find people with the necessary skills, knowledge and attitudes to get the task done. Be sure the make up of the group reflects the range of people who will be affected by the team's work. The recruitment grid is an excellent tool to assess the human resource needs of committees and boards. It is often used by the Nominating Committee as it recruits new board members for the organization.

Recruitment grids help to ensure that the composition of the group will provide the experience and perspective needed to do the work. The far left column of the grid is a list of skills and helpful characteristics that can be developed by thinking about the work of the specific group for which you are planning to recruit. The top line of the grid has the names of all the people currently on the committee. Checkmarks are used to identify the skills each person brings and what will be lost when that person's commitment is completed. Target your recruitment efforts in those areas where you are lacking expertise or representation.

Geography

> lives in Community A
> lives in Community B

Knowledge/Experience

> board or committee work
> finances
> fundraising
> health care
> government relations
> legal matters
> community development
> promotion and marketing
> planning
> organizing

You may want to ensure an even mix of men and women in which case you add "Sex (Female-Male) to the list. Similarly, different age or ethnic groups may appear on the list to ensure that the perspective of these groups is part of the committee.

Bringing new blood into your group infuses fresh ideas and perspectives. Contact people who have not previously participated. People may be flattered that you asked, even if they say no. This recruiting gives you a chance to talk about your group's activities. Use a positive approach. "I have an opportunity for you..."

Encourage diversity to assure a wide variety of opinions, options and perspectives. The most successful groups are those who do not see members as duplicates from the same cookie cutter! Members may take longer to come together as a group but the results will be more productive and effective.

Recruitment Grid

Name of Committee: **Publicity Committee**						
Name of the person currently on the Committee:	Sue	Sam	Joe	Mary	Lori	Yan
When is each person's term over?	'93	'94	'93	'95	95	'93
The skills and experiences we need on this Board/Committee:						
Contacts in Community A	✓					
Contacts in Community B						✓
Interest in the cause		✓		✓		
Planning skills		✓				
Facilitating meetings					✓	
Writing skills				✓		✓
Media contacts or interest in developing media contacts		✓	✓			
Making arrangements					✓	✓
Knows about marketing and promotion						
Radio announcements			✓			

3. Give people a task they want to do!

Think about your own hobbies. Does someone need to urge you to do them? Never! Involvement with a group or committee should be a satisfying way to spend time. Ask people what they like to do. Try to ensure that at least some of the member's needs are met by the assigned task!

One tool that can help people share their hopes and dreams for their involvement is the "Window of Work" concept developed by Dr. Ivan Scheier. It encourages people to "open" their windows of work, is fun and often insightful.

Here's how it works. The "Window of Work", as illustrated in the following diagram, is simply three vertical columns drawn on a sheet of paper. The first column is titled "Skills to Offer", and is the place for the committee member to list all those activities, gifts, interests and skills that the person likes and would willingly offer to do for the group. The second column is titled "Areas for Growth" and is the place to list activities, interests and skills that the person would like to learn. It represents a potential area for personal growth. The third column is "Things to Avoid", those things that the person absolutely does not want to do.

Distribute copies of the Window of Work at your initial meeting, asking people to complete and bring them to the next meeting. At the beginning of that meeting, break into groups of three and have people share with each other their preferences. Follow this with a large group discussion about the value of the varying talents that people bring and how they will enrich the committee work at hand.

Try to design an appealing committee job for each person that uses some of their identified skills and also provides an opportunity to develop at least one growth area. Be sure to collect the Windows and use them to better understand your team's preferences and dreams. People's preferences change over time, so it is important to revisit and update this at the end of each planning cycle as well as annually.

THE WINDOW OF WORK*

Member's Name: **Date:**

Skills to Offer	Personal Growth Areas	Things to Avoid

* Adapted from the work of Ivan Scheier

4. Build trust and rapport among the team members:

Allow time for group members to get to know each other and you. Spend time learning about their backgrounds, what they bring and willingly share with the group. Acknowledge all contributions as potentially useful and valid. Support early efforts to decide how the group will work together. Discover what each member needs to feel included in the work of the team.

Keep people personally connected so they are part of the action and you can hear their concerns. Be sure that all members feel they are important to the group's success. Phone committees that keep in touch regularly are valuable. Consider assigning a buddy to a new group member. Use a team approach whenever possible.

5. Clarify and blend committee members' expectations and needs:

Ask people what they want to accomplish with the group. Point to areas of overlap and easy agreement. Don't be afraid of areas of disagreement, but rather encourage the group to explore these thoroughly, looking for opportunities to resolve differences:

- ♦ are areas of compromise possible?
- ♦ do other forums exist to deal with the issues raised?
- ♦ can the idea be directed to someone for reflection and response?

Spend time harmonizing and checking out what you think you have heard. The effort expended here will reap enormous benefits later.

6. Support the development of mutually held, clearly defined goals:

This step comes more easily if everyone is aware of the wishes of the others. Make sure objectives are specific, measurable, achievable and consistent with the group's mandate. Identify realistic timelines that are communicated to all involved. Use them to monitor progress.

7. Identify activities that lead to the achievement of goals:

Brainstorm a wide variety of possible activities. Encourage people to be wildly creative. Don't rush in at this stage with reasons why the plans won't work. Only after exploring a variety of possible options should you select one. Establish some criteria to measure which ones to choose.

8. Define individual member roles and responsibilities:

Assign specific activities so they feel part of the action and the leader doesn't end up doing all the work. Involvement breeds satisfaction. Experiment with shared leadership and flexibility in work assignments. Don't assume you know the kind of work someone wants to do. Keep in mind the importance of matching work to personal interests, skills and preferences.

9. Find out what direction and coaching people need or want:

Remember the old saying, "different strokes for different folks". Just as different plants require different amounts of light, water and care, so do team members. Ask people individually about what kind of supervision they like best. Do they want a lot of freedom, do they want someone who sticks close and calls often, will they shout when they need help? Clarifying people's preferences with respect to supervision makes for open communication and prevents assumptions and misunderstandings.

10. Establish reporting systems that are practical and helpful:

Even though others may be assuming primary responsibility for getting the job done, the leader should establish checkpoints to keep track of the progress and to determine if the group members are on target. The information may be in written form (reports, checklists, mid-course evaluations) or verbal, which is more informal - "How's it going, what help do you want or need?" The monitoring system you choose will depend on the:

- complexity of the task
- timeline available for its completion
- experience of the group member
- preferred style of supervision requested by the member

11. REDEFINE STRATEGIES, ROLES, COURSE OF ACTION AS REQUIRED:

Work in progress often has to be fine tuned or sometimes fundamentally altered to adapt to changing conditions. Be prepared to be flexible. It is not a failure to abandon plans that aren't working for you. It's a sign of adaptive leadership! Be sure everyone is informed of mid-course corrections and understands what that means for their work. Use meetings to "take the pulse" of the team and to brainstorm together possible strategies to re-direct work currently underway.

12. RECOGNIZE INDIVIDUAL AND TEAM CONTRIBUTIONS:

Celebrate your victories, no matter how small. People need encouragement, especially when things aren't going well or when plans change. Recognition is most effective when viewed as an on-going process that finds people doing something right. A simple thank you can have a big impact. You might want to open each meeting with a celebratory comment about progress to date or a significant achievement. This not only recognizes accomplishments but also sets a positive tone for the meeting.

The role of the chair is not to do the work and determine the outcome of all decisions. The effective chair is a mobilizer of others, recruiting members wisely for their skills, knowledge and interest. The chair encourages, monitors and supports the work of the group and thereby ensures the success of the committee initiatives.

REFERENCES

1. Tuckman, Theories and Models in Applied Behavioral Science, *Volume 2 Group*, 1991. Pfeiffer, W.J. pp 99-103

CHAPTER NINE
NURTURING INDIVIDUAL MEMBERS

WELCOMING FUNCTION

The wise chairperson is sensitive to individual needs. She assures welcome and inclusion by introducing new members and seeking their opinions so that they are encouraged to fully enter the group. The chairperson makes sure orientation takes place and takes responsibility for re-introducing information into the group to allow the new members to feel fully aware of the background which influences decision-making. This is also an important function necessary when visitors or experts join the group even for a short period.

WARM-UPS

Part of the welcoming role involves creating a warm climate that helps people feel part of the group. Warm-ups help people make the transition from earlier activities into the meeting itself, learn more about each other and build a sense of team. The following ideas will help you plan to "break the ice".

RAGGEDY BEGINNING:

Do away with that uncomfortable first person to arrive syndrome. This activity is a great incentive to encourage members to be on time and it also involves them from the moment they arrive. It's a wonderful way to get the juices flowing for the meeting. Select an interesting topic for discussion that relates to the agenda or has relevance for the group.

Write instructions for the exercise on flipchart paper and post prominently where people enter. The instructions might look something like this:

- Find one or two people whom you don't know well
- Discuss the following question for the next 5-10 minutes
- What was the most energizing meeting you ever attended? What made it so?
- Be prepared to share the highlights of your discussion when the meeting convenes

When you initiate this type of beginning exercise, you will find that not only do people start arriving early, but those who get there when the meeting was scheduled to start observe so much energetic conversation that they feel they have arrived late and missed the fun! This is an especially effective way to begin a larger gathering where you expect that many people will not know each other and so will feel uncomfortable at the beginning.

OUT OF PURSE OR POCKET:

This ice breaker is particularly appropriate for a new committee or a smaller group of participants. Ask people to select something from their purse or pocket that has meaning for them and then talk about why they chose that item. People should offer only what they feel comfortable sharing.

If you as the leader share something personal, others are more likely to follow your lead. You will be amazed at the richness of the talents, interests and creativity of the folks around the table. A sense of team and personal respect is developed as people share their feelings and ideas. Be sure to thank everyone and to acknowledge every contribution as you go around the table.

FORCED CHOICES:

This type of exercise can be great fun and is a constant revelation about the incredible interpretative power of images. Choose an appropriate question that forces people to make a choice from several options. For example:

"When I think of myself as a group member, I believe I most closely resemble a..."

- mother bear
- eagle
- ostrich
- owl
- chameleon

Prior to the meeting post these titles (or better yet, drawings) at various points around the room. Introduce the activity with comments about the purpose of the exercise and the value of understanding one's own or others' personal styles. Once people have decided which image to choose, they move to that area and together talk about why they made that choice. The language, images and qualities they attribute to their choice will astound you! After 5-10 minutes bring people together, asking a few to share why they chose a particular animal.

Some people may find it difficult to choose. The number of choices you allow will depend on the number in the group and the time you have to hear back from folks. You'll want to give people time to reflect on the importance of this exercise. It points out how differently we view things, the power of words, the rich imagery we carry, the need to be sensitive to others. Have fun with other questions and images too.

SIMILARITIES AND DIFFERENCES:

Divide people into groups of four, preferably with people they do not know well. Provide each group with a piece of newsprint on which you have drawn a large rectangle. People are instructed to introduce themselves, and to discuss ways in which they are similar as well as different. Before they begin, highlight a range of dimensions that might be discussed: physical traits, attitudes, interests, hobbies, careers, dreams, values, worst nightmares. Similarities are recorded inside the rectangle, differences are noted outside the rectangle, in each of the four corners.

At the conclusion of the exercise, people are encouraged to reflect on the exercise and to value and validate the differing perspectives and skills that people bring to the group. This is a splendid exercise to do with a diverse group because you will find things that bind you together. It also points out profound differences in people who appear to be very similar.

HUMAN BINGO:

This is a fun variation for an ice breaker. Each person receives a bingo "card" with squares that describe whatever characteristics are appropriate for your group.

For a group of municipal staff the squares may read "regularly use cafeteria", "works in recreation", "has five years experience", "union member", "provides information", etc. People move about meeting others and getting other's signatures in the appropriate squares. The first person to get a diagonal X or a cross wins. Be sure and have fun prizes. These bingo cards can be tailored to any kind of group. The physical activity energizes the group in a positive way.

The number of possible warm-up activities is limited only by your imagination. Remember that these exercises provide you with an opportunity to better understand the people in your group. They also help each member of the group feel comfortable, learn who else is there and at the same time share their uniqueness with the group. When you enable people to relax and in a non-threatening way help them learn more about each other, you set the stage for a successful meeting.

HUMAN BINGO

I exercise regularly	I have a grandchild in diapers	I'm a white knuckle flyer
I love to cook	My favourite pastime is reading	A perfect holiday involves travel
I prefer classical to rock	I love the cottage during the summer	I'd rather be outdoors
My birthday is this month	I can speak more than one language	I'm living with teenagers
I look forward to retirement	I love the theatre	I can drive a manual transmission automobile/ truck

Understanding Motivation

In addition to creating a warm climate, welcoming requires an understanding of why people are involved with the committee or group. Marlene Wilson, in her landmark book, *The Effective Management of Volunteer Programs*[1],describes researchers' David McClelland and John Atkinson's theory that there are three different forces that act as motivators to human behaviour. They believe that while most individuals have a mix of all three types, one tends to dominate. The three types identified are:

- ❖ **The Achiever:** This person is committed to accomplishing goals, welcomes a challenge and looks for opportunities to test out new skills and improve performance.

- ❖ **The Affiliator:** This person values relationships, enjoys working with others and seeks out opportunities to be helpful and supportive.

- ❖ **The Power Person:** This person seeks to influence people and events so that change is realized.

No one style is better than any other. In fact, most successful projects require a mix of styles to blend the work of a group. Teams made up of a variety of styles benefit from the different perspectives people bring to the task. People with different styles, however, prefer different kinds of supervision, recognition and job placement. It is helpful to understand a person's preferred style in order to match the person most appropriately to a task.

In attempting to explain the differences among the three styles you might think of the example of the person who joins a Toastmaster Club.

The Affiliator would suggest that she joined because she enjoyed the people in the group and looks forward to the luncheon meetings. She might choose to be on the social committee.

The Achiever joined so she will be more confident in her various leadership roles and would like to win the award for best new member performance.

The Power Person plans to run for political office and would like to persuade the Toastmaster Club members to support her campaign. She is especially interested in environmental issues.

The charts in this chapter outline the motivational types, their positive attributes and some of the possible negative consequences of each type. Remember that people are rarely one type to the exclusion of all other characteristics. They are much more complex than this guide would suggest.

It is important to note that in our culture, there is real discomfort with the notion of "power". Its presence is often noted as a criticism rather than a compliment. McClelland in a later work, "The Two Faces of Power"[2], described power in two ways:

PERSONAL POWER:

This is our more negative description of power. The individual wants to be in charge, the boss. She is more motivated by personal ambition than the welfare of others. This person prefers associates who will be submissive and responsive to her vision of reality.

The individual who is motivated by a need for personal power views power as a finite commodity. By sharing power, information or control with you, that person fears she has less power for herself.

SOCIAL POWER:

This is a more positive view of power. The individual exercises power for the benefit of all. She wants to make changes to help others. There is a genuine concern for the welfare of all players on the team. Some of our greatest world leaders and politicians would be found in this category - Mother Theresa, Martin Luther King, Gandhi, John Kennedy, Jean Vanier, for these people believe power is infinite. In sharing power, information or control with you, these people believe we are all stronger.

As you review the charts more carefully you will discover some of the challenges faced by leaders as they try to work with people of a different motivational type:

The person who is an affiliator is looking for a patient, chatty leader who really cares about how he feels about the group. The leader who is an achiever is just anxious to get on with it.

The affiliator is concerned about any conflict, while the achiever is so focused on the goal that perhaps he is unaware of conflict within the group.

The affiliator may perceive criticism as a personal attack rather than a simple suggestion directed at enhancing results. The achiever believes that everyone is anxious to improve performance and would welcome such a suggestion.

Both the affiliator and the achiever may find the power person too honest, forthright and "pushy".

The power person loves political intrigue, the affiliator hates it.

The affiliator prefers a chair a who attends to the needs of the group. The decisions are secondary. The achiever is happy only if the agenda is covered, decisions are made and the meeting ends on time. Power people only come to the meetings that they think are worthwhile. Yours may not be one of them.

THE IMPORTANCE OF MOTIVATIONAL TYPES FOR LEADERS

We need to understand our own styles and the potential negative attributes that may be misinterpreted by those with whom we work. We also need to appreciate the styles of others and make allowances or modifications in our own behaviour to make all team members feel comfortable and confident. Some suggestions for harmonizing styles:

- Talk openly about differences in style.

- Ask people about their preferred supervisory style and be sure to demonstrate an effort to deliver that kind of support.

- When new groups form, have people talk about motivational styles and their own expectations. Establish mutually agreed upon ground rules that address style issues.

- Ask someone who is a distinctly different style to coach you in meetings or on projects. An affiliator vice-chair who agrees to monitor the process of a meeting can be a real asset to an achiever or power person.

- Look for compromise opportunities to meet a variety of motivational needs. A work meeting of ninety minutes that has a clear, tight agenda will appeal to those who are task-oriented. This can be followed by an optional leisurely social time that will appeal to those people with strong affiliation needs.

- Place people in positions that complement their motivational needs. Someone who longs for social interaction will prefer working with a group, not taking on a task in a back office. Use people's best skills and interests.

- Make your own needs known. If your concerns are pleasantly presented, most people are prepared to work with you when recognition is made of the value of different motivational types.

- Welcome different approaches to problems and solutions. Comment on the value of different perspectives. Leave a clear message that different is desirable.

- Be patient, someone else may be confused or frustrated by your style.

Motivational Type: Achievement

Goal: Success in a situation which requires excellent or improved performance

Description	Conditions of Supervision	Recognition
Positive Attributes: • Concern with excellence/personal best • Sets moderate goals, takes risks • Enjoys a level of moderate stress • Restless / innovative • To be challenged • Likes to work alone • Likes to overcome barriers Negative Attributes: • Will sacrifice people to achieve goals • May be insensitive • Can be autocratic • Gets bored quickly	• Wants concrete feedback to improve performance • Likes results focused management • Wants a boss who leaves him/her alone • Likes to be challenged • Enjoys time management and responds to goals / objectives & conceptual thinking • Needs a well delegated task • Enjoys being consulted about decisions, planning	• Appreciates pins, certificates • Letters of recommendation to the boss • Name mentioned re: achievement of a specific goal • Promotions - increasing challenges • Training to improve performance • Efficient meetings • Letter from the President • Knowing results • Evaluating the results for improvement

Motivational Type: Affiliator

Goal: To be with others, to enjoy mutual friendships

Description	Conditions of Supervision	Recognition
Positive Attributes: • Seeks out relationships • Likes to work with many people • Likes social activity for its own sake • Sensitive to feelings, needs / wants of others • Supports others in achievement of their goals • Talks about feelings Negative Attributes: • Will sacrifice project goals to keep people happy • Concerned about personal popularity • Hates to discipline • Is crushed by criticism	• Wants a concerned, caring supervisor • Enjoys long chats • Welcomes advice • Likes to be part of a team, pair, group • Needs help if situation is tense or unpleasant • Avoids conflict • May not report problems back to supervisor or may "dump" them back to supervisor	• Enjoys sharing success with others • Likes to have family and friends included • Feels a project is successful if friendships have developed • Would highly value compliments from a supervisor - thank you note - pins/plaques • Would feel personally slighted if not recognized • A great party would be an appropriate acknowledgement

Motivational Type: Power People

Goal: To have an impact or influence on others

Description	Conditions of Supervision	Recognition
• Concern for reputation, position, respect • Tries to shape opinion • Wants to change things • Combative, fighting spirit • Verbally aggressive/forceful Personal Power (Negative) • I'm in charge • I win - you lose • Group is dependent, submissive • Treats people indifferently • Autocratic Social Power • Exercises power to benefit others • I win - you win • Charismatic • Creates confidence in group that they are able to achieve goals	• Clear cut policies and procedures • Limits of authority • Likes strong leadership • Needs lots of personal freedom and respect • Work well alone • Tends to operate outside standards rules and regulations • Likes to associate with other "power brokers" • Needs to be included in decision-making and planning	• Public recognition • Opportunity to meet others with power • Media recognition • Being part of the action • Titles • Opportunity to innovate • Work with government

This exercise is particularly useful for leaders preparing to chair committees. It will help people discover their preferred motivational style and promote discussion among group members to increase their understanding.

Briefly introduce McClelland's theory that three different forces act as motivators, acknowledging that although most of us are a mix of all three types, one tends to dominate.

Ask people individually to complete the Motivational Analysis that follows. When finished, they score their answers and mark whether each answer was Power, Achievement or Affiliation. They should then tally the numbers for each motivating force.

Lead a full group discussion on the results. Share with the group more information about the three types.

If time permits, break into groups of like types, and discuss the following questions:

> 1.What kind of direction do you prefer when you are assigned work to do?
>
> 2.What kind of recognition is most welcome?
>
> 3.What advice do you have to help others work effectively with your particular motivational type?

Give groups about twenty minutes to discuss before reporting back to the larger group.

Hand out copies of the Motivational Type Charts and conclude with a full group discussion of the importance of understanding motivational types for committee members working together.

KEY CONCEPTS:

- ❖ No one style is better than another.

- ❖ Effective teams benefit from a mix of styles.

- ❖ Individuals are a mix of styles but one tends to dominate.

- ❖ People's motivational styles may change over time.

- ❖ Different styles prefer different kinds of tasks, support and recognition.

- ❖ Determining one's preferred style can lead to an enhanced committee experience.

- ❖ An understanding of styles allows people to adapt their own styles to make all team members feel confident and comfortable.

Motivational Analysis

Each of the following questions has three choices. Choose the one in each question which most closely fits your own motivations. Remember, there are no wrong answers. Place an "X" before the letter of your choice.

1. _____ a. When doing a job, I seek feedback.
   _____ b. I prefer to work alone and am eager to be my own boss.
   _____ c. I seem to be uncomfortable when forced to work alone.

2. _____ a. I go out of my way to make friends with new people.
   _____ b. I enjoy a good argument.
   _____ c. After starting a task, I am not comfortable until it is completed.

3. _____ a. Status symbols are important to me.
   _____ b. I am always getting involved in group projects.
   _____ c. I work better when there is a deadline.

4. _____ a. I work best when there is some challenge involved.
   _____ b. I would rather give orders than take them.
   _____ c. I am sensitive to others - especially when they are mad.

5. _____ a. I am eager to be my own boss.
   _____ b. I accept responsibility eagerly.
   _____ c. I try to get personally involved with my superiors.

6. _____ a. I am uncomfortable when forced to work alone.
   _____ b. I prefer being my own boss, even when others feel a joint effort is required.
   _____ c. When given responsibility, I set measurable standards of high performance.

7. _____ a. I am very concerned about my reputation or position.
   _____ b. I have a desire to out-perform others.
   _____ c. I am concerned with being liked and accepted.

8. _____ a. I enjoy and seek warm, friendly relationships.
   _____ b. I attempt complete involvement in a project.
   _____ c. I want my ideas to predominate.

9. _____ a. I desire unique accomplishments.
   _____ b. It concerns me when I am being separated from others.
   _____ c. I have a need and desire to influence others.

10. _____ a. I think about consoling and helping others.
    _____ b. I am verbally fluent.
    _____ c. I am restless and innovative.

11. _____ a. I set goals and think about how to attain them.
    _____ b. I think about ways to change people.
    _____ c. I think a lot about my feelings and the feelings of others.

Source Unknown

Motivational Analysis (cont'd)

1.	a.	Achievement
	b.	Power
	c.	Affiliation
2.	a.	Affiliation
	b.	Power
	c.	Achievement
3.	a.	Power
	b.	Affiliation
	c.	Achievement
4.	a.	Achievement
	b.	Power
	c.	Affiliation
5.	a.	Power
	b.	Achievement
	c.	Affiliation
6.	a.	Affiliation
	b.	Power
	c.	Achievement
7.	a.	Power
	b.	Achievement
	c.	Affiliation
8.	a.	Affiliation
	b.	Achievement
	c.	Power
9.	a.	Achievement
	b.	Affiliation
	c.	Power
10.	a.	Affiliation
	b.	Power
	c.	Achievement
11.	a.	Achievement
	b.	Power
	c.	Affiliation

CHEERLEADING FUNCTION

The chair keeps an eye on the goal of the group and reports on progress towards the goal. This is the cheerleader function. It is easy to lose sight of progress and to feel discouraged about the lack of movement forward. By identifying even the simplest steps forward, the chair can help the group over difficult obstacles. One facet of this cheerleading function is coaching.

COACHING: LEARNING TO EMPOWER OTHERS

As chair you have a unique opportunity to be a mentor and coach to those on your team. Your role is to empower all people in the group, encouraging them to take increasing measures of responsibility for their own actions and increasing involvement in the decisions that affect them and the group. Rather than concentrating on controlling people, effective coaches put in place systems that support risk taking and innovation.

These days people expect a relationship between leaders and group members that is characterized by:

- more professional approach to recruiting members
- broader role in decision making
- people with professional skills to offer
- expectation to enjoy their work and make a difference
- more selective willingness to get involved
- acknowledgement that their needs are respected
- chance to be creative, approaching a task as they see fit.

WHAT DO EFFECTIVE COACHES DO?

- enhance the competence and confidence team members
- support efforts
- build and maintain positive working relationships
- clarify goals and objectives
- remove obstacles to achievement of goals
- offer training (mostly on the job)

The actions that one observes in successful coaches include setting standards, clarifying purpose, unifying actions, creating alliances, respecting past traditions, listening, rewarding positive behaviours and setting the task in the frame of reference of team. The skills that make for effective coaching are outlined in The Coaching PACT[3].

> *Let's suppose that you are the President of the Board of a local association. Marlene is the Chair of your Fundraising Committee. She calls you, feeling very discouraged about the commitment of her committee members to get out and raise money as well as her chairing skills. People are not willing to take responsibility for acting on decisions but prefer to leave the work to her. Attendance at meetings is poor and those who come lack energy or enthusiasm.*

WHAT DO YOU DO?

Your meeting with Marlene is the ideal opportunity to practise your coaching skills. Your role is not to tell her what to do, but to help her make decisions and then take action. Coaching uses a variety of skills that you will want to tailor to her need in this situation. By carefully planning your coaching intervention (the meeting), you can offer Marlene broader and more thoughtful support.

The Coaching PACT is a tool designed to help you plan the meeting (coaching intervention) with Marlene. Refer to the completed form illustrated that follows the PACT description.

The Coaching PACT
Purpose - Activities - Concepts - Tomorrow

1. **PURPOSE** of this intervention:

2. **ACTIVITIES** most appropriate for this situation:

   ☐ Listening
   ☐ Clarifying, Restating
   ☐ Building trust (attending)
   ☐ Posing alternatives
   ☐ Reflecting other points of view
   ☐ Facilitating the exchange of resources
      ☐ Person power   ☐ Equipment
      ☐ Money   ☐ Knowledge
      ☐ Tools/techniques
   ☐ Delegating
   ☐ Problem solving
   ☐ Conflict resolution
   ☐ Training (1:1)

   Strategies:

3. Key **CONCEPTS** to be communicated:

4. **TOMORROW**

   ☐ Systems and supports to strengthen this member:

   ☐ Improvements that will benefit other group members:

The Coaching PACT
Purpose - Activities - Concepts - Tomorrow

1. PURPOSE of this intervention:
To enhance Marlene's ability to chair, build her skill, problem solve, offer resources, listen to her frustration, hear what's been tried

2. ACTIVITIES most appropriate for this situation:

- ☑ Listening
- ☑ Clarifying, Restating
- ☑ Building trust (attending)
- ☑ Posing alternatives
- ☑ Reflecting other points of view – Committee members
- ☐ Facilitating the exchange of resources
  - ☑ Person power Bob   ☑ Equipment
  - ☐ Money   ☑ Knowledge
  - ☑ Tools/techniques
     ↓ great books
- ☐ Delegating
- ☑ Problem solving Process Check
- ☐ Conflict resolution   1. Group Mem's handbook
- ☑ Training (1:1)   2. Mining Group Gold

Strategies:
1. Listen to full picture
2. What has she tried?
3. Group stage – what is expected.
4. What else might she try – her ideas.
5. Direct to Bob, excellent CHAIRING skills

3. Key CONCEPTS to be communicated:
- Notion of group development stages
- Involvement = ↑ participation
- role of chair to involve – not solve
- confidence in her – need to review

4. TOMORROW

☐ Systems and supports to strengthen this member:
① attend next meeting with Marlene
   Pre-plan → de-brief. VIDEOTAPE?
② Set up follow up DATE to review
③ Share article on group development
④ Results of Process Check – see
   EVALUATIONS – discuss

☐ Improvements that will benefit other group members:
- all new chairs would benefit from start up training
- build in tips for INVOLVING silent members.

How to Use the Coaching PACT
Purpose - Activities - Concepts - Tomorrow

The form is designed to help you plan a coaching intervention with a group member who needs help. The specific help needed will be different in each situation. Let's look at each component of the PACT form:

Purpose of this intervention:

The coach identifies what she is trying to do. There may be several purposes at play at the same time. Some are unclear as you plan but may develop during the interaction itself. Remember, the role of the coach is not to DO - to solve the problem, to resolve the conflict or to answer all of the questions. Rather, it is to "enable" the group member to do it.

Activities most appropriate for this situation:

The PACT form lists coaching behaviours, with space for you to briefly note your potential responses for any activity. See the sample PACT form illustrated.

Listening: The bedrock of coaching, listening is part of every intervention. You are listening for content, feelings, unanswered questions and confusion.

Clarifying: The coach asks clarifying questions to ensure he understands what has been said. These additional questions may bring new insights to the member.

Building trust: What can the coach do to demonstrate acceptance of the persons's feelings and confidence in her ability to successfully complete the task?

Posing alternatives: The successful coach helps the person broaden potential responses to any situation. Rather than becoming stuck with a single position, he asks "If we did this, what would happen?" By exploring a range of options, the coach helps the person select the best possible response to the situation.

Reflecting other points of view: The coach encourages the member to consider the opinions, feelings and perspective of others involved. This gives her all the needed data to make a wise decision to proceed.

Facilitating the exchange of resources: Can the coach direct the member to someone who has wrestled with a similar problem? What tools or techniques might be used to influence the desired results? Is there equipment or technology that might be useful? For example, might we videotape the next committee meeting for review by Marlene and the coach? Knowledge might include where to find information - a policy book, an article in a professional journal, a video on meeting management.

Delegating: Assigning a project or problem to a member for action. The coach may initiate the interaction, clarifying what needs to be done, under what conditions and by what date. Much of the difficulty in effective delegation comes from the failure to CLEARLY outline the desired results.

Problem Solving: Is the problem statement clear and complete? Do we have all the data we need to suggest alternatives? Are all possible solutions explored?   Are criteria set for selecting a solution? Are concrete action steps outlined? Is responsibility assigned? Is a date for evaluation in place?

Conflict Resolution: What is the issue? What need does it attempt to address? What does the other party in the conflict want or need? What are the barriers to resolution? Can they be accommodated? What other options exist? How might these be most successfully presented?

Training: Is there a gap in knowledge, skill or attitude that can be filled with some training? How might this be accomplished?

Strategies: The member with the help of the coach outlines a step-by-step approach to implement the selected activities, listing possible alternatives. Creating a sequential action plan is helpful.

KEY CONCEPTS TO BE COMMUNICATED:

The most important ideas you want to share with the person. Keep the concept list short to ensure understanding and retention.

TOMORROW:

Systems and supports that will strengthen this member:

This section focuses on making sure the results of the coaching session are acted upon and that the person has the help needed to apply the concepts successfully. Examples of future supports would be assigning an experienced chair as a buddy or a follow-up phone call.

Improvements that will benefit other members:

In offering support to an individual, a coach often identifies a resource that would be helpful for all members. She might also note a gap in current practice that could be remedied. For example, offering an inservice training on meeting management would be useful for all members of the board.

The final component of the cheerleading function that needs attention by the chair is recognition of members' participation.

Look for many **informal** ways of saying thanks.

Be sure that the recognition is **appropriate** to a person's **needs**.

User Friendly recognition reflects your understanding that what may be perceived as positive by one person, may be very uncomfortable for another. Asking a member to give a speech at your annual meeting may be a reward for one person and sheer punishment for another!

Personalized recognition is based on that old truism "different strokes for different folks."

Creatively appropriate recognition responds most effectively to people's needs. Picture a meeting in which a particularly astute member asks tough questions that energize the whole group. The issues needed to be discussed, but you are aware that the person is uncomfortable about other people's reaction. As chair, you should acknowledge the value of that role. Begin the next meeting by presenting that person with a small box of chocolate covered raisins with a note "Thanks for raisin' the tough issues!" This not only supports the individual, but it provides an opportunity to discuss with the group the value of diverse opinions.

Recognition that **meets felt needs** will be very effective. Let's suppose the newly appointed vice-chair of your committee has indicated a desire to improve her meeting management skills. Providing her with an opportunity to attend a facilitation skills workshop acknowledges the importance of her role and contribution.

Develop a **year-round plan** for recognition, acknowledging that it is an ongoing process.

CREATIVE RECOGNITION IDEAS

Develop a plan to recognize people throughout the year and at different stages of their involvement with the group.

AT THE TIME THEY JOIN AS A MEMBER

- A welcome letter from the President of the organization.
- Assign a buddy or mentor to provide personal support.
- Wrap up a miniature flashlight with a note " Welcome to a bright light".
- A package of tea saying "Since you've joined our group, things are really brewing!"

ON A REGULAR BASIS DURING OR BETWEEN MEETINGS

- Take time to talk and smile
- Telephone to say "we missed you".

AT A MEETING

- Review objectives and celebrate accomplishments.

ON AN ANNUAL BASIS

- Special events, pot luck suppers, social activities.
- Annual update of service and fund-raising results.
- Collage of candid photos of all members displayed at an annual meeting.

UPON COMPLETION OF A SPECIAL ASSIGNMENT

- Fill a wine glass with candy and attach a card with the message, "A Toast to a Job Well Done!"
- A box of chocolate Ovations, "Take a bow, you deserve a standing ovation!"
- A glue stick with a note "Thanks for holding us to-gether" or "Thanks for sticking with us."
- A packet of Aspirin with a note: "Thanks a lot. I know it's been a headache."

ON SPECIAL OCCASIONS IN THE MEMBER'S LIFE

- Send a card for birthdays, on the anniversary of being a new member.

- Something meaningful to them personally as a reminder and invitation to return.
- Exit interview that affirms their contribution and seeks their wise advice.
- Letter of reference highlighting accomplishments and contribution.

FACILITATING FUNCTION

The purpose here is to give everyone a chance to shape and influence the group process. Opinions may vary widely and be strongly felt. The chairperson is not expected to behave as Solomon and contribute the "best solution", but can identify the impasse and ask the group to generate the solutions. A helpful comment in this kind of a situation is: "Where are we folks? Where do we want to be?" The chair's role is not a platform for personal positions, but a place to mirror all the thoughts and feelings of the group. This suggests that the best chairperson is a good LISTENER.

THE FACILITATOR'S ART

> "A good leader is best when people barely know that he leads. A good leader talks little, but when the work is done, the aim fulfilled, all others say 'We did it ourselves'."
> - Lao-Tse Chinese Philosopher

The most vital part of creating great meetings depends on effective facilitation. Don't be put off by the fancy term. The word comes from the Latin word facile, meaning "easy". Very simply, facilitating means making it easier for a group to reach its goal.

Bob Kelsch[3] describes a facilitator as "a neutral servant of people". He went on to describe how a facilitator works.

"Guiding without directing; bringing about action without disruption; helping people self-discover new approaches and solutions to problems; knocking down walls which have been built between people while preserving structures of value; appreciating people as people."

The very essence of a good meeting is not structure, or well drafted agendas, but the ability to get people talking with one another and to assist people to shape effective strategies to move them to their desired outcomes. Facilitation is not for the timid. It calls on people to face their feelings and to take risks to be truly responsive and creative. Much of the joy of facilitation, however, comes from the fact that it is a task clearly shared with all group members. The facilitator acts only if others fail to perform the needed functions.

CREATE AND MAINTAIN A WARM AND TRUSTING CLIMATE

To spark full participation, everyone must feel comfortable in the group and confident that all contributions will be valued.

The first part of any meeting is critical to set the tone and to permit people to move into the committee environment. A well-organized, welcoming start makes people glad they've come, while a disorganized beginning suggests that the outcomes are not important.

TIPS TO CREATING A WARM CLIMATE

1. Prior to the meeting, provide name tags or tent cards with names written in large script.

2. Arrive 25-30 minutes early to set the room up in a friendly configuration. Try to arrange the furniture so that all people can see and hear one another. Grouping people at small tables may promote small group discussion if the total group is more than 15.

3. Welcome people as they come in. Introduce them to others. Call people by name.

4. Offer refreshments.

5. Consider posting a welcoming sheet. A flexible beginning that gets people talking about the issues of the meeting as soon as they arrive rather than waiting for a formal start, is a great involvement technique.

Sample instructions:

- Welcome to the first meeting of the Mayor's Task Force

- Help yourself to coffee

- Introduce yourself to at least four other individuals

- Tell them a bit about why you are here

- Describe your hopes for our Task Force

Even with groups where people know each other or have met previously, a "warm up" period is valuable. This is relaxed time when people reconnect with one another and re-focus on shared concerns. Additional warm-ups are described in this chapter.

When formally starting the meeting, the facilitator

- expresses his pleasure at seeing the group

- validates the history and accomplishments of the group to date. This step is exceptionally important. The group grows in confidence when its past performance is acknowledged. Sometimes there is a sense of failure or lack of progress that surfaces when a group reconvenes. It is a time to celebrate past achievements and to welcome new challenges

- shares a bit about his own reason for involvement

- provides an opportunity for each group member to introduce himself to the full group.

Focus group activity on definition and accomplishment of goals and objectives.

The facilitator sends out a proposed agenda that outlines his sense of the purpose and desired outcomes. Group members prepare for the meeting with the purpose clearly in mind. It should sharply focus their reading, thinking and developing of thoughtful questions prior to the meeting.

When the meeting begins, the purpose is re-affirmed as to its continued relevance. Once agreed upon, the purpose is put on flipchart paper and posted. There it serves as the committee's "true north". Use it:

- when there is confusion or conflict to clarify next steps;

- as a summary of work to date, accomplishments;

- to plan the next meeting agenda.

Prior to the meeting, when the facilitator selects the activities, discussion groups and questions to be dealt with, he does so always in the context of the goals and objectives to be achieved. What stands in the way of our achieving our goals? What gaps exist in our information? What are the sources of tension or conflict that must be resolved? What needs to happen next?

The facilitator develops a plan for the meeting that is reflected in the agenda design. In the actual running of the meeting, he acts as a weathervane or thermometer, observing what is happening, assessing how people are feeling and determining whether the plan is meeting the needs that now emerge. If there is a gap between what is happening and what is required, the facilitator re-adjusts the design, offering another option for action to bring the group to its desired results.

The flexibility to respond on the spot to current conditions is greatly aided by the technique "the performance check" [4]. Any group member can stop the action of the group to:

- examine progress towards achievement of goals
- assess group climate
- air feelings, conflict, observations
- evaluate the session so far

Examples:

"Let's call a time out, folks. I think we need a performance check here. We've been re-visiting these same two points for some time. Are we ready to vote on this resolution or do we need further discussion?"

"I'm sensing we're evenly split on how to proceed. Let's do a performance check at this point. How many of you would support extending the meeting for twenty minutes? How many want to end at the pre-established time?"

Once you have a reading from the whole group, you can select an exercise or activity to move forward, confident that you and the group are in agreement.

HELP TO KEEP THE PROCESS ON TRACK:

A return to the purpose and performance check are both useful in keeping the group on track.

Sometimes the process can be diverted for very valid reasons, to introduce new information that must be considered, to review a decision when conditions have changed or to explore an unconsidered option. Sometimes a group member may pursue a personal agenda that causes him to lead the group from its stated purpose. The facilitator can encourage the member to link his comments to the desired result, or can re-direct his comments by getting group support to return to the proposed agenda.

The facilitator need not make that decision unaided. It is appropriate to point out to the group the choice point and the implications it has in any discussion.

Example:

"Bob feels we are not yet ready for the writing of our recommendations. Harold feels we should move ahead now. What's the sense of the group?"

PRESENT AND RECEIVE INFORMATION , FEELINGS AND OBSERVATIONS IN A VARIETY OF WAYS:

One of our most enduring images of how groups work is that of people sitting around a table. Too many groups believe that the only way to work is in a full group. Many decisions and discussions are better served by having people work in pairs, triads or smaller groups of 4-6.

In assigning tasks to sub-groups, four phases are important:

1. Clear instructions given verbally, in written form and posted on flipchart paper.

2. Adequate time allowed for the sub-groups to wrestle with the questions proposed.

3. A report-back opportunity that engages the full group. There are numerous ways to capture the small group work discussion. Different options include:

- posting all comments on flipchart paper and allowing all the groups to walk around and view all responses

- asking each group to contribute on one key comment

- highlighting the key learnings from each group in a verbal report

- using a computer and printer, process all comments to be shared with all participants

- assign report development to a team that will consolidate all feedback and present it at a later time

4. A debriefing session with the full group that explores common themes, summarizes key points and determines how the group will use this information. There is often a reluctance to revisit small group reports, feeling that all that has been said is enough. The last step encourages people to make meaning of the subgroup work so that the impact can be felt in group deliberations.

MONITORING FUNCTION

One of the most terrifying tasks for the new chairperson is the monitoring and control of "difficult" committee members. The chair is expected be a traffic cop, restraining the dominant and often opinionated member and encouraging hesitant group members to be heard.

A WORD ABOUT THE DOMINANT PERSON

While all difficult behaviours are a monitoring issue for the chair, the challenge of the overly talkative or dominant person is particularly vexing. Chapter Three earlier described a number of excellent strategies, including the point-counterpoint and "black hat" approaches. Additionally as chair, it is possible to interrupt by establishing eye contact, by raising your hand to indicate "stop", by interjecting with "Thanks, let's see how other people feel about that ...", or even by physically touching if the person is seated nearby.

A final technique that can be a fun way to deal with the issue is a concept called "Spend a Penny".

Each person in the group is allotted three pennies. They may be actual coins, artistic cards or even creative tokens. These "pennies" become the currency for participating in group discussions. To express a point of view or to expand on the discussion at hand, people must "spend a penny" to be accorded the right to speak.

This technique balances group involvement by forcing the more vocal folks to think twice about jumping in with a comment, lest they quickly spend their pennies and from then on be unable to participate. At the same time quiet members may become more involved and add "their two cent's worth".

Introduce this exercise sensitively, making it a fun process to promote discussion rather than a gimmick to point fingers at the dominant few.

Terminal Niceness

Far too often people suffer through endless meetings, frustrated that the personally-focused needs of a few members prevent the group from generating more productive outcomes. Dealing with these difficult people and problems requires skill and tact.

Leaders, especially those with strong affiliation needs, are often uncomfortable about confronting disruptive behaviour. We are conditioned to avoid conflict, to sweep strong feelings under the rug, to smile and pretend that things will improve or that the person will mercifully be transferred to another city!

This situation is particularly true in voluntary groups and nonprofit organizations where we somehow expect that people will work harmoniously together for important causes. Our fear of hurting people's feelings and our reluctance to address these behaviours directly creates a climate of "terminal niceness" 5. This "smiling on the surface" atmosphere at meetings results in guarded communication and the avoidance of conflict at all costs. We believe that the time has come to cure this terminal niceness syndrome.

Ideally a group will see all members monitoring their own and others' behaviour. Most often, however, this responsibility falls to the chair. The following descriptions of "meeting types" identify nine common behaviours and why they may occur. Your effectiveness as a chair will increase significantly when you add these strategies to your meeting management toolbox.

Responding to Common Meeting Problems

1. Behaviour	Reasons Why	Possible Solutions
Person **dominates** the discussion, is overly **talkative**	• eager beaver • wordy by nature • well-informed • show-off • lonely, needs to feel accepted	• interrupt with ... "That's a point, what do other people think?" • ask others for different perspectives • interrupt and summarize • interrupt and indicate that comments are not related to discussion • seat near you to be responsive to body language • call a straw vote
2. Behaviour	**Reasons Why**	**Possible Solutions**
Person is argumentative, overly **aggressive**	• feeling pressured, upset • aggressive personality • argumentative by nature • has not been acknowledged • has been dismissed or ignored in the past	• do not get angry as well • summarize valid points made, then move on • solicit group support by asking if others agree, then move on • talk to person privately, try to develop cooperation • seat beside you so that you can more easily control
3. Behaviour	**Reasons Why**	**Possible Solutions**
Person is **dictatorial**, wants own way, makes decisions without committee	• may not know how to delegate • believes own way is best • needs power • very controlling nature	• ask for input from other members • talk with person privately • do not establish eye contact • encourage expression of opinion, then move back to the group

Responding to Common Meeting Problems

4. Behaviour	Reasons Why	Possible Solutions
Person is a **discourager**, always responds negatively to new ideas	• long-time member may feel has tried all ways • may be threatened by new people, ideas • may want to cling to power of "tradition"	• encourage person to share why it didn't work • use humour to defuse discouragement • acknowledge past experience • be supportive of the other members' ideas
5. Behaviour	**Reasons Why**	**Possible Solutions**
Two people have an **argument**	• each believes other is wrong • strong/directing personalities • can split group	• emphasize points of agreement • refer to meeting objectives • request input from another member • ask a specific question related to topic • request personal issues be withheld
6. Behaviour	**Reasons Why**	**Possible Solutions**
People having a **side conversation**	• may be related to subject, but person has not been recognized to speak • may be personal comment • may be "Doubting Thomas" • may be the perennial "down putter"	• direct a question to one of the people involved • intervene and remind that only one person has the floor • encourage people to use a note pad so as not to lose thoughts • keep a pad to record order of speakers and enforce it • interrupt, restate last remark made by group and ask person's opinion of it

Responding to Common Meeting Problems

7. Behaviour	Reasons Why	Possible Solutions
Person who promises to do something and **doesn't follow through**, often misses meetings	• procrastinates by nature • unable to set realistic goals • has good ideas, can't put into practise • lack of confidence • may not know how to do task	• be sure person understands what is expected • set guidelines/timelines mutually • offer support • talk promptly, one-to-one about attendance • inform person before meeting that a report is due
8. Behaviour	Reasons Why	Possible Solutions
Person who **rambles**, talks about irrelevant issues	• wants attention • loses train of thought	• thank person and summarize what was said • interrupt, remind what objective is and move on • appoint an observer to assess participation • ask person to briefly summarize • smile, comment that point is interesting, but must move on to topic being discussed • refer to time allowed for discussion of issue.
9. Behaviour	Reasons Why	Possible Solutions
Person who is very **quiet**, does not contribute to the discussion	• may be shy by nature • may simply not have anything to say • may be there but really "on holiday" • may not be clear about expectations re participation	• seat near you, look for cues that indicate he might like to comment • check at break to affirm his opinions are sought • if aware of a helpful point made in another context, ask if she will share that with the group

Tips for Improving Your Chairing Skills
A Final Summary

Ensure that the physical set-up facilitates interaction.

The fastest way to sabotage group participation is to have a seating arrangement that excludes people or has them sitting with their backs to others. Ideally the set-up should accommodate people sitting comfortably around a squarish or round table, so that they can maintain eye contact with each other. Try to avoid a long, narrow table because it prevents good communication. The room should be large enough to allow people to break into smaller groupings for meaningful discussion. If the room is very crowded, you may need to arrange for break-out rooms.

Be sensitive to non-verbal communication

Be sure to place yourself where you can see how people react to suggestions, speakers' styles and decision-making plans. Watch for facial expression, body language and shifts in posture that indicate a strong reaction. Check out your observation by asking for feedback.

Encourage everyone in the group to participate

Be attentive to silent members, looking for clues that they might be prepared to contribute to the discussion. Check with them during a break and affirm that their opinions are sought. Try to limit dominant members by suggesting..."Let's hear from some others, please". Protect members who appear to be under attack. Humour sometimes works well here. "Whoa, that's a mighty powerful statement. I'd like some other reactions to that......"

Discuss what is meant by group norms and why they are needed

Establish some group rules at the beginning of the task together. What about reports, absences, starting on time, how voting will happen, confidentiality, smoking? There are many unspoken rules that people should have a chance to make explicit. Discussing them openly and agreeing as a group to these ground helps members become responsible for monitoring their own behaviour.

RESTRICT YOUR PARTICIPATION IN THE CONTENT DISCUSSION

As chairperson, refrain from expressing opinions on items for discussion. Your job is to listen intently and to summarize and rephrase what you have heard as direction for action. Encouraging diverse views is important. "Who could give us a different perspective on this issue?" If you feel very strongly about speaking to an issue, withhold your comments until other people have had an opportunity to express theirs. Before sharing your views, indicate that you are no longer wearing the "chair's hat", but that of an interested member. Remember that the position of chair carries significant weight for many people. Others may be swayed by your position more than by the persuasiveness of your arguments. In the longer term, this does not build a creative team. Decisions made by the group should not be reversed by the chair or by staff after the meeting. This totally undermines people's participation and commitment to the goals.Encourage regular group evaluation

Ask how people feel about both the content and process of the work you are doing together. Simply ask, "How are we doing? What did we accomplish today? What is our major task ahead? What might we have done differently? How are we working together as a team? Are we listening to one another yet?"

ENCOURAGE OTHERS TO TAKE THE LEAD

The most productive groups evolve when members are encouraged to share leadership in planning meetings, leading discussions, gathering data, and resolving disputes. As leader you are trying to wisely use the resources of the group. Build on the expertise from within the group but don't hesitate to bring in external help if the group feels it doesn't have the knowledge or skill to handle a problem.

Once the group has achieved its goals it may well be time to disband. Groups need frequent infusions of new blood to keep creative. People seem to prefer work groups or task forces that have a short life span. Remember that "a time to come and a time to go" is the best prescription for members, leaders and healthy groups.

And so this book comes full circle - from participating as an effective group member, through the enhancement of chairing skills, to ultimately empowering others to join us in a productive and shared leadership. We wish you and your group the satisfaction of saying "Together we did it!"

> *If you want one year of prosperity, grow grain.*
> *If you want ten years of prosperity, grow trees.*
> *If you want a hundred years of prosperity, grow people.*
> *Chinese Proverb*

REFERENCES

1. Adapted from a description of the work of David McClelland and John Atkinson in Marlene Wilson's *The Effective Management of Volunteer Programs.* Volunteer Management Associates, Boulder, 1976.
2. Ibid
3. Mackenzie, Marilyn and Moore, Gail, *The Volunteer Development Toolbox,* Heritage Arts, 1993
4. Bob Kelsch, quoted in *Mining Group Gold,* a personal communication with the author, Thomas Kayser.
5. MacKenzie. Marilyn, *Curing Terminal Niceness...A Practical Guide to Healthy Volunteer/Staff Relationships,* Heritage Arts, 1990.

BIBLIOGRAPHY

Abbey-Livingston, Diane and Kelleher, David, *Managing for Learning in Organizations: The Fundamentals*, Government of Ontario, 1988.

Abbey-Livingston, Diane and Wiele, Bob, *Working With Volunteer Boards: How to Improve Their Effectiveness*, Government of Ontario, 1984.

Bellman, Geoffrey, *Getting Things Done When You're Not In Charge*, Bard Books, 1992.

Bone, Diane, *The Business of Listening*, Crisp Publications, 1988.

Carver, John, *Boards That Make a Difference*, Jossey-Bass Publishers, 1991.

Covey, Stephen R., *Principled Centered Leadership*, Summit Books, 1990.

Covey, Stephen R., *The 7 Habits of Highly Effective People*, Simon & Schuster, 1989.

De Bono, Edward, *Six Thinking Hats*, Penguin Books, 1985.

Fisher, R. and Brown, Scott, *Getting Together*, Penguin Books, 1988.

Haynes, Marion E., *Effective Meeting Skills, A Practical Guide for More Productive Meetings*, Crisp Publications Inc., 1988.

Heider, John, *The Tao of Leadership*, Bantam Books, 1988.

Johnstone, Ginette, *Chairing a Committee, A Practical Guide*, Johnstone Training and Consultation, 1989.

Kayser, Thomas A., *Mining Group Gold*, Pfeiffer & Company, 1990.

Kim, W. Chan and Mauborgne, Renée A., "Parables of Leadership", *Harvard Business Review*, Volume 70, Number 4, July-August 1992.

Kouzes, James M., Posner, Barry Z., *The Leadership Challenge,* Jossey-Bass Publishers, 1990.

Mackenzie, Marilyn, "Creative Followership", *Voluntary Action Leadership,* Spring 1989.

MacKenzie, Marilyn, *Curing Terminal Niceness...A Practical Guide to Healthy Volunteer/Staff Relationships,* Heritage Arts, 1990.

MacKenzie, Marilyn and Moore, Gail, *The Volunteer Development Toolbox,* Heritage Arts, 1993.

Mandel, Steve, *Effective Presentation Skills, A Practical Guide for Better Speaking,* Crisp Publications Inc., 1987.

Nolan, Timothy, Ph.D., Goodstein, Leonard, Ph.D., Pfeiffer, J. William, Ph.D., J.D., *Plan or Die!,* Previously published under title *Shaping Your Organization's Future,* Pfeiffer & Company, 1993.

Phillips, Steven and Elledge, Robin, The Team Building Source Book, University Associates, 1989.

Theories and Models in Applied Behavioral Science, Volume 2 Group, Pfeiffer, William J. Editor, 1991.

Von Oeck, Roger, *Whack on the Side of the Head,* Warner, 1983.

Wilson, Marlene, *The Effective Management of Volunteer Programs, Volunteer Management Associates,* 1976.

Yarbrough, Elaine, *Conflict Management,* Heritage Arts, 1988